THE CONCISE GUIDE SERIES

a concise guide to

Supervising a Ministry Student

Ann M. Garrido

Kevin E. McKenna, Series Editor

ave maria press AMP notre dame, indiana

THE CONCISE GUIDE SERIES

The Concise Guide Series, edited by Kevin E. McKenna, tackles questions of central importance for contemporary Catholicism. Each book in the series carefully outlines the issues, references the necessary documents, and sketches answers to pressing pastoral questions.

© 2008 by Ave Maria Press, Inc.

All rights reserved. No part of this book may be used or reproduced in any manner whatsoever, except in the case of reprints in the context of reviews, without written permission from Ave Maria Press®, Inc., P.O. Box 428, Notre Dame, IN 46556.

Founded in 1865, Ave Maria Press is a ministry of the Indiana Province of Holy Cross.

www.avemariapress.com

ISBN-10 1-59471-179-8   ISBN-13 978-1-59471-179-4

Cover and text design by John R. Carson.

Printed and bound in the United States of America.

Library of Congress Cataloging-in-Publication Data
Garrido, Ann, 1969-
  A concise guide to supervising a ministry student / Ann M. Garrido.
    p. cm. -- (The concise guide series)
  ISBN-13: 978-1-59471-179-4 (pbk.)
  ISBN-10: 1-59471-179-8 (pbk.)
  1. Pastoral theology--Fieldwork--Supervision. I. Title.
  BV4164.5.G37 2008
  253.071'55--dc22
                            2008019883

This book is dedicated to Charlie—

who died a thousand deaths for the good of the whole.

CONTENTS

Chances are you are reading this book because you have been invited to supervise a ministry student. That alone is powerful testimony. Someone obviously has a great deal of respect for you and your ministry or you would not have been asked to consider taking on this role. An equally powerful testimony is that you have now cracked the cover of this text, indicating that the invitation to supervise is something you take seriously. You are willing to invest time and energy in finding out about and readying yourself for the role. Only one paragraph into this book and it is clear that about 75 percent of what it takes to be an excellent supervisor is already in place in you.

The remaining paragraphs of this book are dedicated to exploring the other 25 percent. They seek to build upon the foundation of quality ministry and serious commitment that already exists by introducing "nuts-and-bolts" information about ministry supervision and the topics frequently engaged in the supervisory relationship.

Chapter 1 offers an overview of field education in Catholic ministry formation. It introduces field education principles and terminology common in current ministry formation documents.

Chapter 2 introduces the structure of field education that helps maximize the learning of the ministry student. It includes information about preparing for the formal field experience to begin, developing a learning contract, and preparing an evaluation.

Chapter 3 explores the key learning method in field education—theological reflection. Theological reflection is a "buzzword" in a variety of venues, but this chapter will speak about its potential specifically within field education.

Chapter 4 raises several issues that frequently surface in the supervisory relationship. It offers helpful hints and resources for engaging these issues.

Chapter 5 looks at the spirituality of the supervisor. While the heart of this book is about the supervision *of* ministry, it should be acknowledged that this kind of supervision *is in itself* a ministry. As such, supervision is more than a task; it is a call, a way in which God seeks to draw us nearer and forms us into the persons God dreams us to be. This chapter looks at how supervision is a praxis—a self-transforming activity.

Each chapter ends with several questions for reflection and discussion. These questions may serve as personal preparation to enter into the role of supervisor, but they are probably best utilized in group conversation with other supervisors. Many ministry formation programs are discovering that supervisors learn and grow and flourish as supervisors when they have the opportunity to meet regularly with others who engage in the ministry of supervision.

In the appendices of this book, you will find further exercises that could be helpful in developing supervisory skills, including sample case studies, scripture images, and a supervisory self-evaluation. Again, these exercises could be engaged either individually or in peer groups with other supervisors. The appendices also contain relevant selections from current ministry formation documents that guide the work of field education in Catholic circles in the United States.

Because ministry formation at this time in our history involves a great diversity of persons, including both men and women, I have chosen in this book to use both masculine and feminine pronouns when referring to students, supervisors, and directors of field education. I realize that it can be awkward when reading to have the pronoun continue to alternate, but hopefully it will not distract and instead serve, in a small way, to keep before us the many faces of ministry in our Church. I have also sought to include examples and case studies from field education that represent the wide variety of ministries for which students prepare and the variety of lifestyles that support them—lay, ordained, and vowed.

Much of what is included in this book has been gleaned through my experience as a field education student and later as the field education director at Aquinas Institute of Theology in St. Louis, Missouri. I will remain forever grateful to this institution for all of the ways that it has helped me grow as a minister. It is the best "placement" that any ongoing learner could ask for. In particular, I want to thank those who have served in the field education department with me: Michael Stancil, Sharon McKinnis, Carolyn Wright, Celeste Mueller, Greg Heille, and the more than forty wonderful supervisors whom we call upon year after year. I also want to express my appreciation for my colleagues in the Catholic Association for Theological Field Education (CATFE) and the National Association for Lay Ministry (NALM) Ministry Formation Directors Institute, who have opened my eyes to the many different settings and ways in which the promise of field education is being lived out in Catholic ministry formation programs in both the United States and Canada. Finally, I acknowledge my husband, Mike, whose fifteen years of ministry in parish administration and now Catholic health care have provided more wonderful grist for reflection than any field education director could hope for. The case studies we have processed together have been the most life-changing of all.

Ann M. Garrido

An Introduction to Ministerial Field Education and Supervision

Field education is perhaps the oldest method of ministerial formation in the Judeo-Christian tradition. Even from the time of Moses and Joshua or Elijah and Elisha, we see a pattern of mentorship emerging in which new ministers learned their profession through years of one-on-one tutelage with an experienced minister. Education took place not in the confines of a lecture hall but on the barren plains of the Sinai desert, the slopes of Mount Nebo overlooking the Promised Land, and the palaces of Ahaziah. In the gospels, we find that after a period of time observing Jesus teach and heal, the disciples were immediately sent out to announce the nearness of God's reign and to cure the sick. On their return, they talked about their experiences with Jesus, tried to figure out what these experiences meant, and praised God together. Following Christ's resurrection, the earliest ministers of the Church were formed by the close relationships that they shared with apostles and Christian leaders from other communities. We find the example of Paul, who took under his wing a number of young future leaders and missionaries including Timothy and Silas. And, we have the witness of Priscilla and Aquila, who received the preacher Apollos into their home and built upon his already solid knowledge of Jewish scripture and the message of Jesus to offer a fuller picture of what it meant to live in the resurrection with the baptism of the Spirit.

After the close of the apostolic era, ministry formation continued in much the same way. While there is some evidence of Christian scholars beginning to study together during the Patristic period in schools at Alexandria and Edessa, these institutions were primarily catechetical and theological in nature. Candidates for the emerging ministerial priesthood, by and large, were formed in the cathedrals, where they might assist the bishop and older priests for any number of years before being ordained themselves. As they passed through a variety of minor orders, their duties would increase gradually until they became experienced in reading and explaining scripture, instructing catechumens, celebrating the sacraments, and guiding communities of faith. Augustine of Hippo formalized a communal mentoring relationship with his first *monasterium clericorum*, a house next to the cathedral where priests could live with one another and learn from each other's experience. Such cathedral communities existed through the Middle Ages, but they were truly viable only in urban settings. In rural areas, the mentoring of new church leaders remained much more individualized and, in some areas, did not happen at all.

While there were many strengths to mentorship as *the* method of ministerial formation, there also proved to be some problems. Over time, the lack of a consistent, theologically substantive, and unified approach to formation led to a great deal of ill-informed and often erroneous preaching and teaching within the church. While the rise of universities in the twelfth century helped increase the theological understanding of some church leaders, only about 1 percent of the clergy were able to take advantage of university courses.[1]

The experience of the Reformation shook the Catholic Church to its very core. At the Council of Trent (1545–1563), which met in response to the Reformation, one of the most sweeping changes that the Church made was in the area of priest formation. For the first time, seminaries were established in each diocese to offer a coherent and theologically substantive formation for ministry. Formation became much more academically oriented as students began to study from textbooks under learned scholars. Soon, formation for ordination took place almost exclusively within the confines of the seminary, quite separated from the daily life of the Church in cathedrals and parishes. Protestant traditions, too, placed a priority on well-educated leadership, often affiliating with or creating universities to offer rigorous theological training. In the United States, the first universities— Harvard, Yale, Princeton, and Dartmouth—were all founded originally as divinity schools so that the fledgling nation would be assured highly trained ministers.

In the centuries following the Reformation, however, both the Catholic and Protestant traditions learned an important lesson. Just as field learning and mentorship alone do not always produce the best ministers for the Church, neither does purely academic learning. Persons can have a tremendous amount of theological knowledge and still lack all pastoral wisdom and relational skills. The strongest formation for ministry requires a combination of both theological study *and* practical, pastoral experience. It requires great learning but *also* reflection upon that learning in light of the daily life of the Church in the world. It requires instructors, *and* it requires mentors. Some things are best learned in a classroom. Some things are best learned in the field.

Modern ministerial field education has its roots in the educational developments that took place in this country in the late nineteenth and early twentieth centuries. At that time, law and business schools, such as Harvard's, began to experiment with using actual experiences from the fields of law and business as the beginning point for study and learning, rather than theoretical texts. Students were encouraged to discover the relationship between what they learned in the classroom and real-life incidents. They were urged to see how theory could be applied in the practice of the profession, but also how the practice of the profession could give rise to new theory. The success of the experiment led other professional disciplines to shift their teaching methodology as well. Soon medical and social work schools were developing "clinical" learning opportunities for their students. Divinity schools would not be far behind.

In 1935, the American Association of Theological Schools—a body of both Protestant and Catholic seminaries that sets common standards for academic accreditation—established a committee to look at the possibilities that clinical education might hold for ministerial formation. Over the next several decades, seminaries began to incorporate field experience into their schools' curricula. Through a process of trial and error, experimentation, and reflection on that experimentation, schools slowly learned what worked and what didn't and shared their learning with one another. Much was gleaned from the wisdom of ministers involved in an effort called clinical pastoral education—an emerging program for the formation of pastoral care ministers set not in a seminary at all but rather in the hospital. In 1956, the persons who oversaw the field experience portion of their schools' curricula began to gather regularly to promote further study and sharing about the new evolving discipline, now called field education. The Association for Theological Field Education (ATFE) was born. In 1981, Catholic members of this organization began to caucus with one another to address issues specific to the Catholic tradition. Thus the

Catholic Association for Theological Field Education came into being.

Field education is now a required component of ministerial formation in all seminaries accredited by the Association of Theological Schools (ATS).[2] Moreover, recent ecclesial documents reiterate the expectation that field experience will be part of all Catholic ministry curricula, whether affiliated with ATS or not, and even whether affiliated with presbyteral ordination or not. Since the Second Vatican Council, there has been a proliferation of Catholic ministry formation programs to serve a burgeoning diversity of ministries within the Church, many of which are now being undertaken by deacons and lay ecclesial ministers as well as priests and vowed religious. Some of these formation programs continue to be set in the context of the seminary, but many are also sponsored by universities, colleges, religious communities, health care institutions, and diocesan offices. Recent publications from the Vatican and the United States Conference of Catholic Bishops (USCCB) make clear that these programs, too, are asked to integrate field education within their curricula.[3]

From these ecclesial documents, we can learn a great deal about what the Church understands field education to be at this point in its history, why it believes field education is important, and what it hopes that field education will do. Key insights include:

FIELD EDUCATION IS NOT THE SAME AS FIELD WORK

In the early days of introducing a field component to seminary formation, sometimes field education and volunteerism were seen as synonymous. Students were sent "to help out" in a parish or hospital or school. They might go to the pastor or principal and ask what needed to be done or how they could be of use. Volunteerism is a wonderful thing, but it is not the same as field education. The primary aim of volunteerism is service of the site (the parish, hospital, etc.). The primary aim of field education is growth of the student as minister. In field education, the student comes with something that she wants to learn. The ministry that she does at the site is specifically constructed to serve that learning. Hopefully, in her learning, the site will always be served, but the focus is on the student's education. The *Program of Priestly Formation* states very succinctly, "Whatever the setting, it is necessary that it facilitate learning."[4]

FIELD EDUCATION REQUIRES SUPERVISORS

Field education is not field education without the presence of a supervisor—an experienced mentor and evaluator in the field who can help the student grow in the ministry. The term *supervisor* can carry negative connotations in our culture. Sometimes we may have the idea of a supervisor as one who stands by the timecards and watches to make sure people punch in before the bell and don't clock out early. Or, we might think of a supervisor as an inspector, an overseer. Church documents do not talk about supervisors in this way. Rather, a supervisor is a facilitator of learning—one who, with humility and insight, can help craft the experiences the student will have and also reflect on these experiences with him. The three key qualities that the *Program of Priestly Formation* lifts up as essential in supervisors are: experience, competence, and generosity.[5] In essence, the supervisor needs to have "been around the block a few times" so as to help others walk it. He needs to be good at what he does. And he needs to be willing to share not only his knowledge but also his ear and his time with another. Sometimes it is the last one of these three that is the hardest. Often those who are very good at what they do have the least time to teach others how to do it!

Some argue that, given how different the use of the word *supervisor* is in a field education context versus a business climate, it would be better to find another term—such as *mentor* or *reflection partner*. Indeed, some field education programs may choose to do that. It is crucial to remember, however, that the documents call for this person to have an evaluative capacity to his or her role. Unlike someone who is purely a mentor or reflection partner, the supervisor is generally expected to give written feedback on a student's readiness and abilities for ministry. The documents indicate that supervision is a ministry of and for the Church, ensuring that its ministers are well trained and well suited for their work. The documents speak of supervisors as being, in a sense, extensions of the ministry program's faculty.[6]

FIELD EDUCATION REQUIRES REFLECTION

The experience of ministry alone does not a good minister make. We have all known people who have been in ministry for a long time but never seem to grow or learn from their experience. In the words of one elderly priest: "I used to think that I had the wisdom of fifty years of ministerial experience. I now see that I simply had the wisdom of one year of experience repeated fifty times." The difference between "fifty years' wisdom" and "one year's wisdom fifty times over" is theological reflection. It is through reflection on our experiences that we acquire the ability to learn from these experiences, to make changes, to be changed. The documents place a heavy burden of responsibility on reflection, expecting that the habit will "provide an opportunity for personal synthesis, the clarification of motivations, and the development of directions for life and ministry," "enrich spiritual life," "help the development of pastoral skill," and "interpret pastoral experience or activity in light of scripture, church teaching, personal faith, and pastoral practices."[7] Clearly, they do not regard theological reflection as an optional component of the field education experience, but rather a critical element in the effectiveness of the learning process, worthy of significant attention and time.

FIELD EDUCATION TEACHES SKILLS FOR MINISTRY

As noted in the overview of field education's history, there are some ministerial skills that cannot be learned in the classroom. They are best learned in the observation and the doing of ministry. Church documents offer a long list of skills that will hopefully be attained as part of a student's pastoral formation—ranging from administration to listening, from cross-cultural sensitivity to preaching.[8] Indeed, the list is so lengthy that probably no program of study could address them all in a systematic way. But, in the course of field education, opportunities to learn and practice many of the skills that a particular student most needs to work on will have a way of mysteriously presenting themselves. Hence, field education helps the student achieve "a genuine confidence in his own ability—a realistic sense of achieving the knowledge and skills required for an effective ministry. . . . "[9]

FIELD EDUCATION DEVELOPS MINISTERIAL IDENTITY AND AUTHORITY

We have said that there is more to being a good minister than possessing lots of knowledge. One must also possess pastoral skill. Yet even the addition of skill does not complete the picture.

In many jobs, it would. A truck driver, for instance, is an excellent truck driver if he knows and follows the rules of the road, understands the inner workings of his vehicle, and can get it where it needs to go. If he listens to raunchy music while in his cab or hangs out at less-than-reputable bars while he is off duty, these things are not likely taken into account in his annual evaluation and would most likely be considered none of his employer's business. Not so with the minister. Ministry is a *profession*—a term rooted in the ancient religious practice of "making profession." Moral theologian Richard Gula recalls,

> The trademark of being a professional in the classical sense entailed the commitment to acquire expert knowledge and skills and to serve human needs with good moral character. . . . [P]rofessionals are to reflect a high degree of congruence between what they publicly declare to be committed to and the way they carry out their tasks.[10]

Ministry, then, is more than a function within the community; it is also a way of being. Sometimes the development of an appropriate ministerial identity and authority takes a great deal of time. When persons begin to function as ministerial leaders in a community, their status within the community changes, generally in proportion to the amount of commitment, power, and leadership implied by the new role. They are regarded in a different way, whether they want to be or not. New ministers come to recognize that they are public figures, even when they think that they are out of the public eye. They are perceived to represent the Church, and often the voice of God, when they think they are representing only their own view. People treat them with a respect, or sometimes a disrespect, they feel they don't merit. They are included in privileged conversations about the most intimate aspects of people's lives, which they never would have been part of before, and at the same time often are not included in once-familiar conversations with old friends who aren't quite sure how to relate anymore. Rather than serve a personal agenda or mission, they must develop eyes that see the whole, ears that hear the diversity of voices, a heart that loves the many, a mind that makes decisions for the good of all. This requires so much more than an acquisition of skill. It requires taking on a new communal consciousness.

Field education is the place in which important issues regarding ministerial identity and authority can come to the surface. Pope John Paul II spoke persuasively of this dimension of field education when he wrote that the experience could not be "reduced to a mere apprenticeship aiming to make the candidate familiar with some pastoral techniques." Rather, it should be designed to "initiate the candidate into the sensitivity of being a shepherd."[11] His remarks were in reference to future priests, but the language works well for all who are being ushered into leadership positions. All persons who tend to a community need to develop "the sensitivity of a shepherd."

FIELD EDUCATION AIDS INTEGRATION

Field education can play a crucial role in helping ministers integrate the theology and pastoral information that they learn in the classroom with the lived reality of the church and world. In former times, field education was sometimes mistaken for "applied theology." The thought was that the student learned what was important in the lecture hall and then went out and "applied" that learning in the community. In this model, field education was often placed at the end of a new minister's formation, suggesting that it was more of a one-directional endeavor—a transitional period from school to work. Modern field education, however, is understood to be two-directional. Learning flows both from the classroom into the field and from the field into the classroom. Theory and experience are in dialogue with one another and shape one another. Theology is not supposed to be a static discipline but a dynamic one.

As a result of this renewed understanding, field education generally is now located in the middle of or throughout the formation program. Students complete their field education experience either concurrent with course work or interspersed throughout their course work. Field education helps the course work make more sense. It gives study an urgency that it might not have had before; the questions are real because people in the pews are asking them, and the ministry student needs (or at least deeply desires) to find the answers. Field education helps make the student's ministry formation experience a more cohesive one. *The National Directory for the Formation, Ministry, and Life of Permanent Deacons* says that pastoral field education "fosters a general integration in the formational process, forging a close link between the human, spiritual, and intellectual dimensions in formation."[12]

FIELD EDUCATION ASSESSES SKILLS, IDENTITY, AND INTEGRATION

Field education not only helps the student foster new skills, develop a ministerial identity, and integrate learning, it also helps the Church learn about the student's skills, identity, and integration. In short, it assists the Church with assessing readiness for ministry. Field education is where the Church is able to see its candidates for ministry in action. It gives the Church a window into the person-as-minister that simply observing the person in the classroom environment never could. Through the feedback of the supervisor and other persons at the field site, ministry formation programs receive the information that they need to carry out the responsibility entrusted to them by the Church to provide the Church with only healthy, whole, and effective ministers. The feedback received in field education plays a valuable role in the ongoing discernment of a ministerial vocation.

Most of the time, field education feedback truly helps affirm a student's call. Sometimes it helps a student see that she does have a call, but there is still much growth needed to actualize that call. Sometimes it helps students realize that their call is to another kind of work.

Although the examples are fortunately few and far between, many of the ministers who have done the most egregious harm to their communities through sexual abuse or the like were trained in a time when they had either little or no field education as part of their formation. Valuable information that might have been gleaned before ordination, profession, or certification ever took place was not available. The *Program of Priestly Formation* considers the feedback received from field education to be so valuable that it lists it as one of the three "necessary components" of an effective program—along with supervision and theological reflection.[13]

FIELD EDUCATION BROADENS VISION

All of us grow up with an image of the Church and the world shaped by our own life experience. We tend to think, for example, that the Catholic Church we encountered in our parish growing up is representative of the Church at large. We are inclined to believe that the Church has always been the way that we encountered it and should always be that way. When we talk about "the Church," we usually have a pretty narrow sliver of the whole in mind. The same could apply to our vision of the neighborhood, city, or country in which we live. As noted above, however, the minister is called to have a consciousness of the whole, a broader vision. In order to preserve a legitimate diversity and extend the widest possible ministerial embrace, the new minister must cultivate a truly catholic perspective.

Field education offers experiences of diverse populations that the minister-to-be may never have encountered before and, depending on future ministry, may never encounter again. The documents speak of students being placed in interreligious, multicultural, and economically diverse settings. They advocate for experiences in parishes but also beyond.[14] Many students have had powerful experiences in social ministry settings, hospitals and hospices, immigrant outreach programs, schools, jails and prisons, domestic violence and homeless shelters, police departments, and advocacy services. Many programs choose to offer cross-cultural immersion experiences in foreign countries or along the U.S.-Mexico border. Although the student may end up in a very familiar setting after finishing the ministry formation program, she will have an expanded consciousness of issues being faced in other places and can serve as a bridge between her community and the larger Church and world.

FIELD EDUCATION IS SPIRITUALLY ENRICHING

God is at work in the details of our lives—whatever those lives might be. When we are attentive to our experiences, when we ponder them and turn them over in our minds, we gain a greater clarity about what God *is* doing in our lives and what God *wants* to do in our lives. Like Mary in the Gospel of Luke, we are invited to "treasure" the mysteries that life puts before us and reflect upon them in our hearts (Lk 2:19).

All of the above is doubly true when we speak of field education. The experience of ministry is a particularly privileged one. So often in ministry, we are granted the grace to be with people in their most raw moments—times of great laughter and joy, but also times of deepest grief and freshest anger. We are sometimes welcomed into spaces where even family members and close friends are not invited to tread.

Ministry is a place where persons come face to face with what is most essential and, hence, a place where God is especially alive and active. Field education puts students into sacred places, sacred relationships, and sacred moments.

Moreover, field education gives intentional space for reflection on those sacred experiences. The practice of theological reflection establishes a habit of conscious attentiveness to divine activity. We should expect that students will be radically touched by what they see and hear in field education. We should expect that they will see new faces of God and grasp new insights into God's ways. While the student's relationship with God is not the primary focus of field education, we certainly should expect that it will be affected. The *Program of Priestly Formation* explicitly speaks of students emerging from their field experience and reflection as possessing "a better inner sense of direction because of an enriched spiritual life."[15] *Co-Workers in the Vineyard of the Lord* speaks of theological reflection in ministry formation as helping "participants to recognize the movement of God in their lives and ministry."[16]

Summary

In surveying these insights lifted from the documents, two things become clear. First, field education within the Catholic Church has evolved tremendously within the last several decades. To paraphrase a popular automobile commercial: this is not your father's field education experience. The age-old wisdom behind the importance of practical hands-on experience and mentoring has now been wedded with an educational structure involving reflection and evaluation to create a rigorous, effective method of learning. The field education program in which you are being invited to serve as a supervisor is quite possibly more developed than the one to which you were exposed in your own formation for ministry. In several more years, as we continue to learn and refine, it will likely be stronger yet. Field education as a discipline is still evolving.

Second, the Church's expectations for field education are plentiful. Much of what the Church hopes will happen in the pastoral and even spiritual formation of the minister is entrusted to the field education experience. This can be quite an intimidating realization for field education supervisors and program directors alike. How can one field education program address all of the expectations and ideals named in these documents? How does one create an experience that will both be spiritually enriching for the student and promise substantive feedback to the program? How can field education offer a broadening experience of other cultures and faith traditions while at the same time strengthening leadership within one's own particular community?

In reality, while most ministry formation programs acknowledge the potential of field education in all of these areas, they will place priority on some aspects of field education more than others. This is due in part to the particular outcomes and ethos of their program and in part due to the resources and personnel available to them. Some programs will focus exclusively on the development of parish ministers; some will focus on ministries of healing or teaching or service to the poor. Some programs aim for depth and expertise; some seek breadth. Some programs emphasize the learning aspect of field education; others emphasize the evaluative aspect. Some programs may have a full-time director of field education and possibly one or two other persons in a field education department. In many programs, the person entrusted with directing field education will also wear several other hats. Some programs may be located in areas where there are many theologically trained supervisors available; others will serve areas with few opportunities for theological education. All of these factors impact the nature of the field education component within the ministry formation program.

There is no single way to do field education at the present moment in the Church's history, and this is not bad. Varying approaches serve a variety of students and circumstances. As you consider serving as a supervisor, it would be good to speak at length with the director of your student's field program to find out what the program's goals and desired outcomes are. How does the program director understand field education? What are the director's hopes for students in the program? What principles of field education does the program most emphasize? How is the role of the supervisor conceived?

In this book, only a general overview of current field education practices and concerns within Catholic ministry formation programs can be offered, recognizing that the details of each program are unique. A glossary of some common field education "lingo" follows. Individual programs may use alternative terms, but for the purpose of this volume the glossary will help introduce a common vocabulary so that we can explore the world of field education together. Remember that amid the diversity and particularities, you will find all programs consistently have one thing in common: the desire to provide the Church and the world with the best ministers possible.

A FIELD EDUCATION GLOSSARY

Field Education: a learning experience in which a student acquires and tests knowledge and skills applicable to a particular profession by actually engaging in the work of that profession and reflecting upon it. Field education is a common method of education in numerous professions including law, medicine, teaching, social work, and ministry. In this text, all references to field education will be directed toward ministry.

Ministry Formation Program: a program that prepares persons for ministry in the church and the world through human, spiritual, intellectual, and pastoral formation. At this point in time in the Catholic Church, such programs may serve future or current priests, religious, deacons, and/or lay ecclesial ministers. Programs may be set within the context of a seminary, graduate institute, university or college, religious community, health care institution, or diocesan setting.

Director of Field Education: the person who oversees the field education component of a particular ministry formation program. Sometimes this is a distinct role within a learning institution, and sometimes it is an additional role taken on by the administrator of the ministry formation program or one of its instructors.

Field Education Student: the primary "learner" in the field experience. The term does not connote youth or inexperience. In fact, current participants in ministry formation programs span a variety of ages and possess a range of experience. Field education presupposes an adult learning model in which the student's previous life experience is respected and honored and in which the student is understood as the primary agent in his own learning.

Site: the "textbook" of the field education experience, the location and community in which the experience takes place. Potential field education sites for ministers include parishes, domestic violence shelters, hospitals, hospices, schools, nursing homes, food pantries, jails, and crisis counseling centers, among others.

Supervisor: an experienced co-learner and guide who helps the student "read" the site and learn from it. The supervisor is generally responsible for preparing the site for the student's arrival, assisting the student in developing a learning contract, regularly engaging in theological reflection with the student, and writing an evaluation of the student. The supervisor often serves as a liaison between the site and the director of field education. Generally supervisors are on-site, meaning that they themselves serve at the site where the student is serving. Sometimes, however, because of extenuating circumstances, an off-site supervisor may be a better option. This is especially the case if a student is already employed at a site or chooses a site in which there is no suitable on-site supervisor. In this case, the supervisor still works with the student on her learning contract, theological reflection, and evaluation, but is not a regular presence in the student's learning environment.

Placement: the assignment of a student to a particular field education site and supervisor. Placement happens in a variety of ways. Sometimes the director of field education appoints the student to a particular placement. Sometimes the student is expected to initiate the placement. Often the process of placement falls somewhere on the spectrum between these two poles.

Learning Contract: a written agreement among the student, supervisor, and formation program that identifies the student's learning goals, strategies for reaching these goals through the placement, and necessary logistical information.

Evaluation: written feedback provided at the end of the student's placement to help the student, the supervisor, and the formation program look back on the student's learning for ministry and set goals for growth.

Theological Reflection: the act of intentionally making connections between faith and life. In the field education context, theological reflection is any process that specifically helps the student make connections between his theological learning and ministerial experience, with attention also to the role that culture and personal history play in shaping our actions and interpretations.

Questions for Reflection and Discussion

1. What kind of field education experience, if any, did you have as part of your ministerial formation?
2. Which aspects of field education (supervision, theological reflection, skill building, identity building, etc.) were strongest or most valued in your personal field education experience? Which were weaker or less valued?
3. What aspects of field education do you understand to be most important in the program in which you've been asked to serve as a supervisor?
4. Does the summary of contemporary field education in the Catholic Church offered in this chapter alter or expand your previous understanding of what field education is and/or could be? If so, how?
5. If you could identify another aspect of field education not addressed in this chapter's summary of recent ecclesial documents, what would it be? Is there anything important that you feel is missing?

CHAPTER 1 NOTES

1. "Seminary, ecclesiastical" in *Catholic Encyclopedia* [encyclopedia online] (n.p.: The Encyclopedia Press, Inc., 1913; accessed 14 March 2007); available at www.newadvent.org/cathen/index.html; Internet.
2. Association of Theological Schools, *Degree Program Standards*, A.3.1.4.
3. Important recent documents on ministry formation include:
   - *Pastores dabo vobis* (*PDV*)—the 1992 apostolic exhortation from Pope John Paul II on the formation of priests.
   - *Program of Priestly Formation*, fifth edition (*PPF 5*)—the newest edition of norms for priestly formation in the United States, released in 2006.
   - *The National Directory for the Formation, Ministry, and Life of Permanent Deacons* (*NDPD*)—promulgated in 2004 to establish norms for the formation of permanent deacons.
   - *Co-Workers in the Vineyard of the Lord* (*CWV*)—a 2005 document of the United States Conference of Catholic Bishops that describes and suggests elements of formation for lay ecclesial ministers.

   Also important for consideration are the 2003 standards for the accreditation of ministry formation programs established by the USCCB Commission on Certification and Accreditation. All documents are available online through the USCCB website (www.usccb.org). Relevant passages on field education from these documents are found in Appendix E.
4. *PPF 5*, #239 par. 7.
5. *PPF 5*, #240.
6. *PPF 5*, #240.
7. *PPF 5*, #239 par. 7; Ibid; *PPF 5*, #248; Ibid.
8. See commentary on ecclesial documents and USCCB/CCA standards in Appendix E.
9. *NDPD*, #128.
10. Richard M. Gula, *Ethics in Pastoral Ministry* (Mahwah, NJ: Paulist Press, 1996), 13.
11. *PDV*, #58.
12. *NDPD*, #126. See also p. 50 in *CWV*.
13. *PPF 5*, #248.
14. See *PPF 5*, #239 and #246 as well as *NDPD*, #126.
15. *PPF 5*, #239 par. 7.
16. *CWV*, 42.

CHAPTER 2

A Structure That Supports Learning

The primary aim of field education is student learning. As mentioned in the first chapter, we may rightly hope that bringing a field education student on board will also serve other goals. For example, we may hope she will be of good service to the local community or alleviate current staff workload. First and foremost, however, the student is there to learn how to be a better minister. In this chapter, we will look at four processes that most field education programs use to maximize student learning: **making the match, preparing the environment, writing a learning contract,** and **evaluating the experience**. (A fifth process, theological reflection, will be addressed in chapter 3.)

Many programs will have paperwork that accompanies each of these steps. Sometimes students and supervisors will be tempted to regard this paperwork as a burden or "jumping through a hoop." And, indeed, feedback concerning your experience of completing the paperwork with your student should be offered to the program director, but in general, know that the paperwork exists as it does because, over time, it has proven to assist the student-supervisor relationship and deepen the learning experience. At each step, it can be helpful to ask, "How can we use this process and its accompanying paperwork to truly maximize learning?"

Making the Match

Programs use a variety of ways to match students and supervisors. Perhaps your student contacted you directly. Perhaps you were approached by the field education program's director or your religious superior. Perhaps you contacted the program looking for a student intern. Regardless of how the request was made, it is important to meet the student, if at all possible, before committing to the supervisory relationship. The purposes of such an initial meeting are many. First, you will want the student to see the site before committing to it. Does it offer the kinds of opportunities that the student is looking for? The more informed the student is, the less likely the student will need to terminate a placement early. You also want to see whether the student is a good match for the site. Does she seem like the kind of person who would fit in well with the staff? Would he help enliven the kind of ministry that goes on in your location? Do the student's interests match some of the needs of your site? Is she available on the days and times that the ministry takes place?

Second, you will want to make sure that the fit between you and the student is a good one. A good supervisor can work effectively with a variety of different personality types. There is no need to accept only students who have similar personalities or share common interests and ministry styles. At the same time, there is no reason to enter into a relationship that you sense from the start would drive both of you crazy. Some degree of compatibility is essential. Furthermore, you will want to ask, "Do I have what it will take to help this student progress in ministry?"

Persons in ministry generally fall into four categories. Jokingly, we might refer to these categories as "unconsciously incompetent," "consciously incompetent," "consciously competent," and "unconsciously competent." In his book *Multiply the Ministry*, Sean Reynolds more appropriately labels these categories as "the beginner," "the apprentice," "the partner," and "the master."[1] Each of the categories possesses both special gifts and special challenges. The **beginner**, for instance, often brings a tremendous amount of enthusiasm and energy into ministry. At the same time, he doesn't yet know all that he doesn't know. Errors, sometimes on a grand scale, can be common. The **apprentice** knows there is much of what she doesn't know and is often very ready to ask for help and advice. On the other hand, some apprentices are hesitant and overly cautious, even a little fearful, especially if they feel like they've made mistakes in the past. The **partner** comes with a degree of confidence and experience that is a gift to ministry. At the same time, he can be resistant to authority and outside feedback because he has developed enough self-assurance to trust his own insight. He is less likely to take direction without questioning. The **master** is long experienced and can handle complex situations with a sense of clarity and ease. The challenge for the master, however, is that because she has been around for so long, she can be resistant to the ideas of newer ministers. She has seen both too many ideas and too many ministers come and go. She also can become impatient with newer ministers, forgetting all the steps that need to be taken to complete a task because they come so naturally to her after years of experience.

Supervisors generally fall in the category of the master minister. For many the opportunity to supervise is one of the best things that they can do for their own ongoing growth and fulfillment in ministry. Masters need to mentor in order to remain healthy and alive in ministry themselves. Supervising another brings fresh insights, perspectives, and questions, offering the supervisor the possibility of looking at his or her longtime ministry in continually new ways. Supervising helps to make the unconscious conscious and intentional again.

Students, however, do not fall into just one category. Instead, they run the gamut. Some students are genuine beginners to ministry with little experience even at the volunteer level. Other students are coming into formal ministry formation with years of experience in ministry, even at the professional level. As such, different kinds of students are going to need different kinds of supervision. The beginner will require orientation to the ministry. He may need extensive directions and regular follow-up. His ideas may need some "reining in," and his boundaries may need protecting. For example, even if he thinks he can commit to running the youth group alone (and this would be a huge load off of your schedule), he may need you to "protect him from himself." The apprentice will require opportunities for shadowing and lots of availability for answering questions. The partner does not need as much time but rather a certain freedom and independence. The partner needs a more hands-off supervisor who is comfortable with letting the supervisee find her own voice. The master needs a supervisor who will relate more as a peer and help the master reflect on his long-term ministry with a new set of eyes.

Some supervisors find that they work better with one kind of student than another. They may be looking for a partner, but instead find that the inquirer is really a beginner (or vice versa). When meeting with a student for the first time, it can be helpful to get an understanding of the category in which the student sees herself. Then, it is good to know oneself well enough to recognize whether you have the capacity to offer the student the kind of supervision that she needs at this time in her development. Even if the two of you "hit it off" personality-wise, do you have the time to mentor someone brand new to the ministry? Do you have the flexibility to be challenged by a partner who might want to do things differently?

After the introductory meeting, it is good to contact the student within a few days to let him know whether you are willing to commit to the supervisory relationship. In some cases, the student may be interviewing several supervisors looking for the best fit. It is okay to ask the student to let you know by a certain date whether he anticipates working with you or not.

Preparing the Environment

Once you and a student have committed to entering into a supervisory relationship together, several steps need to be taken before the placement officially begins to make sure that it gets off to a smooth start. It is important to alert fellow staff members about the student's arrival, especially if you anticipate the student's working with any of them as part of the placement. Perhaps the student can be invited to a staff meeting or retreat to introduce herself. It is also important, if possible, to alert the community that the student will be serving. In some cases, an announcement can be made in the parish bulletin or the institution's newsletter or a welcome notice can be placed on a communal message board.

A Sample Bulletin Welcome Announcement

An oft-quoted proverb states, "It takes a village to raise a child." Less well known, but equally true, is the ancient practice of our faith community: "It takes a Church to form a minister."

This fall, our *(parish/other)* community has been asked to help in the education and formation of a ministry intern from *(name of ministry institution with a brief description of the institution)*.

(Intern's name) is a *(seminarian, lay minister, etc.)* at *(ministry institution)*. *(S/he)* will be with us for *(one month, nine months, one year)* as part of an internship. While here, *(s/he)* will *(offer a brief description of the intern's proposed ministry)*.

(Intern's name) will be mentored by *(on-site supervisor's name)* while at *(site name)*. However, everyone at *(site name)* is asked to play a role in *(intern's name)*'s learning experience here. Welcome *(him/her)*, introduce yourself, and invite *(him/her)* to share in our community life. *(Intern's name)* *(will be present on the parking lot next weekend after all of the Masses / or other arrangement)*. *(S/he)* can also be reached at *(intern's office phone or e-mail)*.

On a very concrete level, preparing the environment for a ministry student involves consideration of the physical space. Will the student have his own desk? Will she need a dedicated telephone line? Will he have access to a computer? Will he need an institutional e-mail address? If the placement is short term or for a limited number of hours per week, these features are often not necessary, but if the student will be committing a great deal of time on-site, they will help the student settle much more quickly into the placement and will increase the effectiveness of the student's ministry. One of the most common problems field education students report, especially in parish settings, is feeling like the spare piece in an otherwise well-oiled machine. Students can have a hard time getting to meet people and, once they do, without an e-mail address or a phone number, people do not know how to contact them.

In addition, it is critical to alert the student of any special requirements of the site so that these can be taken care of early and not delay the start of the placement. For example, many hospital sites require that the student have a TB test and acquire a volunteer badge. Many settings require drug screenings and criminal records checks. In settings that serve children, one may be required to attend a workshop on child abuse. Some diocesan-sponsored settings require that the student sign a code of ethics. A crisis hotline center may require a daylong orientation. If you serve in a large institution, it is important to let your own employment supervisor and, in some cases, your legal department know that you will be supervising a ministry student. Sometimes in health care or social service systems, a legal department will require an agreement to be signed between the system and the ministry program before a field education student can start. These extra requirements can take longer to meet than first anticipated, so it is good to inform the student early and begin work on meeting the requirements as soon as possible.

Writing the Learning Contract

At the start of a field placement, most programs require the establishment of a learning contract. A good contract can make a world of difference in the effectiveness of a field experience, so it is worth spending at least one and a half to two hours together with the student preparing one. Learning contracts set goals for what is to be learned during the field placement and establish strategies for meeting these goals. They also put into writing expectations that both the student and supervisor have for the relationship so that these are clear as the placement begins. The more clearly the parameters of the relationship are articulated from the start, the less likely that problems will arise over the course of the placement.

At the heart of the learning contract is the establishment of goals. The best goals emerge when students have first had the chance to do authentic self-assessment, considering the goals of the field education program. Many programs have designed self-assessments that can help the student consider strengths and growing edges in relation to the particular goals of the program. In absence of a specific document from the program, the following general assessment may be helpful. Most field education programs share the goals of deepening professional competency, heightening ministerial identity and authority, and developing the habit of theological reflection.

Ministry Self-Assessment Tool

This tool is designed for students preparing to write goals for their field education learning contracts. After evaluating yourself according to each of the following course goals using a scale of 1–5, with 5 meaning "strongly agree," identify four or five areas that you want to work on this semester (or year) in order to grow in your effectiveness as a minister. Discuss with your supervisor to determine how your ministry this semester (or year) could help you to meet the learning objectives you identify.

Professional Competency

____ I possess the knowledge and skills that I need to be successful in my ministry during this field experience. *If no, comment upon what more you would need to know in order to be effective:*

____ My behavior, dress, and demeanor are befitting that of a professional minister.

____ I am able to prioritize among many tasks and successfully negotiate many demands on my time.

____ I am consistently able to meet deadlines.

____ I show up on time to appointments, meetings, and other scheduled events.

____ I plan ahead instead of procrastinating.

____ I am faithful to commitments that I've made. I follow through on things I've said I'd do.

____ I have healthy boundaries and know how to say "no."

____ While maintaining boundaries, I am still accessible and approachable. I also know how to say "yes."

_____ I have established ways to work through stressful times without making the lives of those around me more difficult or burdensome.

_____ I know when to observe and listen and when to become active and speak.

_____ I am not hindered by either high introversion or high extroversion from being a valuable and active member of a group or staff.

_____ I am comfortable going out of my way to introduce myself, to meet new people, and to try new things.

_____ I am able to live comfortably with ambiguity; I do not need to have reality be "black and white."

_____ I am able to bracket my own point of view when necessary so as to listen more fully to another.

_____ I am able to observe confidentiality. I know what to keep confidential and what needs to be reported to a supervisor or another authority.

_____ I am able to work collaboratively with others.

_____ I am aware of what my gifts are for ministry and also my challenges.

Ministerial Identity and Authority

_____ I have a strong sense of being called to ministry.

_____ I feel comfortable with the community regarding me as a minister.

_____ I am aware of the ethical standards expected of public ministers in the Church and am able to live up to them.

_____ I possess a strong pastoral presence in ministry.

This pastoral presence is marked by:

    _____ excellent listening skills

    _____ comfort with silence

    _____ ability to display empathy and compassion

_____ ability to be with those who are grieving or angry

_____ ability to be with those who hold different perspectives than I do

_____ ability to be with persons of other gender / ethnicity / sexual orientation

_____ I possess a strong prophetic presence in ministry. This prophetic presence is marked by:

_____ commitment to justice and peace

_____ ability to confront injustice, irresponsibility, error, and ignorance

_____ ability to offer constructive criticism

_____ ability to negotiate conflict successfully

_____ recognition of the role that suffering plays in ministry

_____ endurance and faithfulness

_____ I am comfortable acting in a leadership role in a community.

_____ I am capable of making decisions, even under stress, even when they do not make all people happy.

_____ I have a good understanding of what healthy authority looks like.

_____ I am unafraid to possess authority and speak with authority.

_____ I have a healthy relationship to those in authority within civil society, the Church, and community life.

_____ I am capable of sharing authority and empowering others for leadership.

_____ I am a "transparent" person; my public persona is not disconnected from my private persona.

_____ I exercise appropriate self-disclosure; I know what to share of myself (and where applicable my family / community life) and what not to share.

_____ I am a person of prayer myself and am comfortable leading others in prayer / praying publicly.

_____ I make choices after considering both the communal impact and the personal impact of my decision.

Habit of Theological Reflection

_____ I come with a strong understanding of theology and theological method that I am able to draw upon with ease.

_____ I see how the theology I have studied connects to everyday life and how everyday life can raise theological questions.

_____ I find myself spontaneously making theological connections in ministry.

_____ I have the capacity to integrate cultural and social analysis into theological reflection.

I understand the ways in which the following affect the ministry I do:

_____ my family history

_____ my personality

_____ my gender

_____ my sexuality

_____ my ethnicity

_____ my personal life experience

_____ I am able to think symbolically—to bring a broad range of images from life, scripture, and history to theological reflection.

_____ I am capable of creative and honest thinking, not dominated by thoughts about how I ought to think or feel; what I ought to say or do; or how another should think, feel, or do.

_____ I am able to identify and articulate what I feel.

Once the student has completed the self-assessment, she can identify four or five areas that need attention. These should form the outline for the goals in the learning contract. In general, it is good to limit the number of goals in a learning contract to about five. If too many goals are developed, it will be hard to give each of them appropriate focus, and there is a danger of no longer holding oneself accountable to any of them. On the other hand, learning goals should be attentive to a variety of areas of ministerial development. For example, they should not all relate to just theological reflection or to just development of professional competency. One experienced former supervisor asked all of his students to write at least three goals: one focused on a new skill that they wanted to learn, one focused on the interpersonal dimension of ministry (i.e., something they wanted to learn to enhance their relationship with others), and one focused on the intrapersonal dimension of ministry (i.e., an aspect of their inner life that they recognized was a hindrance or an obstacle to better ministry).

After the goals are established, the student and supervisor need to work together to consider strategies for addressing and measuring progress toward these goals. This is where the supervisor's knowledge of the site can be especially helpful. You, more than the student, will know what kinds of opportunities are possible in your setting for working on these goals.

Sometimes it is difficult to conceive concrete, measurable ways for addressing the student's goals, especially those that are *intra*personal. Tools like journaling and charting are acceptable, but often promises to keep extensive records of ministerial experiences are difficult to maintain. The bulk of a student's time should be spent ministering with people versus recording experiences with people. Be wary when students want to make radical lifestyle changes as part of their field education contract (e.g., "I will begin to spend an hour a day in silent prayer reflecting on scripture in preparation for preaching," or "I will journal after every visit to a patient"). When strategies require such amounts of time, they are rarely kept, and the contract should contain only activities to which one is willing to be held accountable, or the contract becomes just an exercise in paperwork. It would be better to say, "I will begin reflecting on scripture for ten minutes a day," or "I will journal when I have a patient encounter that leaves me feeling uncomfortable or inadequate." The promise to address an issue as it surfaces in theological reflection is a very solid strategy for many intrapersonal goals. For example, a goal such as this is quite useful: "When I find myself avoiding conflict in a situation, I will bring this situation to my next theological reflection appointment with my supervisor."

Below are samples of realistic and meaningful field education goals and strategies that may help in preparing a contract with a student.

Goal: I am rather shy and would like to become more comfortable in reaching out to people.
Strategies:
- I will be present after each of the Sunday Masses and introduce myself to three new people each time.
- I will go with Sr. Fran on five hospital calls over the course of the fall.
- Once a week, I will visit with the schoolchildren in the cafeteria during lunch hour and make casual conversation with them.

Measurement: I will know if I am making progress in this goal if, at the end of the semester, I feel more comfortable meeting strangers and if I have established a regular ministerial relationship with at least ten parishioners.

Goal: I would like to develop stronger public speaking and teaching skills.

Strategies:

- I will observe Fr. George when he preaches at least five times in the beginning of the year, being attentive to what attracts people to his preaching. I will meet with Fr. George after each event and review the preaching, asking him how he put the preaching together and why he chose to do so as he did.
- I will preach at five Masses for the schoolchildren later in the fall and solicit feedback from several of the classroom teachers after each service.
- I will serve as part of the RCIA team this coming year and lead weekly presentations at least three times. I will ask fellow team members to give me written feedback on my presentations.

Measurement: I will know if I am making progress in this goal if the feedback from the teachers and RCIA team members is positive and if I feel more comfortable in the role of teacher/preacher at the end of the placement.

Goal: I would like to become more skilled at managing conflict during this placement.

Strategies:

- I will read a recommended text on conflict management.
- I will shadow the crisis social worker for several weeks, observing how she handles conflicts that emerge as a regular part of her work. In the second half of the semester, I will try to take the lead in some of the crisis calls to practice conflict management as it is needed. Afterward, I will ask the crisis social worker for feedback.
- If a conflict arises with my supervisor or any other staff member during the course of the practicum, I will not

avoid it but will seek to address it in a straightforward manner, practicing good conflict management skills.

Measurement: I will know I am making progress in this goal if I successfully negotiate conflicts as they emerge in the placement and if, at the end of the semester, I feel less frightened of engaging in conflictual situations.

Goal: I want to develop a deeper understanding of the causes of homelessness so that I can become a more effective advocate for change on this issue.

Strategies:

- I will interview at least five of our homeless clients, recommended by my supervisor, to hear their life stories.
- I will bring a verbatim report of one of these interviews to theological reflection with my supervisor.
- I will interview the two social workers who serve here for more information on homelessness and a bibliography of possible readings on homelessness.

Measurement: I will know I have made progress on my goal by faithful completion of the interviews and theological reflection based on what I hear during them.

In addition to the establishment of goals and strategies, many learning contracts will include a separate section of questions designed to help make clear the parameters of the field education placement. If the contract does not include such, it is still a good idea to talk about parameters with your supervisee. Such a dialogue can help the supervisor and the student uncover expectations of the relationship that the other didn't know existed. Questions for this conversation might include these:

1. What specific duties will the student be held accountable for on-site? To a large degree, these should correspond with the activities delineated in the learning objectives.
2. What is the relationship of the student to other staff members? Does he need to report to or inform any of them about his activities?
3. Are there any financial expectations regarding this placement? Will the student be given a stipend? Will she be reimbursed for any expenses? Does she have a budget?
4. Are both parties clear about the beginning and ending dates of the placement? Are both parties clear about the number of hours the student commits to the ministry? Is the student expected to be present during holiday weeks? During exam week?
5. What kind of supervision can the student expect from the supervisor? Does the student have any special needs or expectations of the supervisor? How often do the student and supervisor anticipate meeting during the placement? Is there a specific time you could put on your calendars now? If a supervisory appointment needs to be changed, how will you let each other know?
6. Recognizing that conflict is present in all healthy relationships, how will the two of you communicate with each other should dissatisfaction or tension arise between you at some point during the placement?

All learning contracts are working documents. After student and supervisee have signed the contract, it should not be filed away in a desk drawer but rather brought out as part of every supervisory meeting. During each meeting, the contract should be briefly reviewed to recall what the student has committed to working on and see how progress is being made. When choosing topics for theological reflection, it is very helpful to choose incidents that are connected in some way to the learning goals in the contract at least some of the time.

Depending on the length of the placement, contracts should be seriously reassessed and revised at least once every four months. In the course of working on goals, it will sometimes become clear that what one thought was a major growing edge is in fact not the real issue. Goals that seemed at first to be interpersonal turn out to have intrapersonal roots. For example, the student who wanted to address shyness discovers that the problem is not a lack of friendliness but a deep-seated fear of being perceived as awkward or foolish. In this case, the next step in working on this goal might be reflecting on where this perception comes from and changing one's self-image. Students and supervisors should feel free to adjust the contract as needed over the course of the placement to better serve the student's learning. Often, in the middle of a placement it is much clearer what the real learning goals need to be.

Evaluating the Experience

At the end of a placement, most field education programs require a formal evaluation of the experience that mirrors the production of the learning contract. The supervisor and student are asked to look once again at the goals created at the beginning of the relationship and assess whether or not they have been met. Students are generally asked to consider what the next steps might be in addressing some of the issues that have surfaced during the placement.

The evaluation experience is an incredibly important part of the overall field education experience and should be viewed as an excellent learning opportunity in and of itself. In a church that has not always placed a high value on structures of accountability, it may be the first time that a student has received written feedback on her performance as a minister, even if she has served for many years. It can be very helpful to receive positive comments and to be able to see how one has grown. It is equally helpful to receive challenging comments and feedback concerning areas for growth. Rather than conceiving of evaluation as punitive, as our larger culture often does, evaluation should be considered a right of the student and a service to the church.

Different programs handle the evaluation process differently. Sometimes students are asked to complete the majority of the evaluation form after consulting with the supervisor. Sometimes the supervisor completes the majority of the paperwork after consulting with the student. Regardless of the process chosen, it is important that the evaluation be honest. Ministry formation programs are responsible to the Church and to society to graduate ministers who are mature, healthy, and competent. Programs depend on field education supervisors to provide accurate assessment of their students.

It is also important that both parties know what has been written on the evaluation. The supervisory relationship is an adult relationship and, as such, it should be transparent. The student should always know what is being reported to her ministry formation program about her. It can be awkward recording challenging comments on an evaluation. Many times it would be easier to give only positive marks and high praise. But offering the student areas for ongoing growth and learning is one of the most valuable gifts that you can give a budding minister. The greatest learning happens when there is both honest, constructive critique as well as affirmation. This having been said, it is important that nothing on the evaluation come as a surprise to the student. If something negative or challenging is to be said to a student, it should not come "out of the blue" but be directly related to conversations that have already taken place earlier in the placement. Ideally, problems are addressed as they surface in the placement and not "filed away" to bring up at the time of evaluation. Evaluation is not the time for new feedback but a synthesis of feedback that has been offered consistently throughout the placement.

Evaluative comments are most valuable when they are based on observed behaviors rather than a judgment concerning attitudes. For instance, it is more helpful to note, "John frequently came to theological reflection appointments without any notes" than to say, "John doesn't value theological reflection." Or "Susan spent the majority of her time on-site alone in her office" versus "Susan doesn't like people." Attitudinal judgments can be dismissed or debated by the other party, but behavioral observations offer something concrete and tangible to work on in the future. It helps students become more aware of how their behaviors are perceived by others, even if that is not what they intended to convey.

Even though it is the nature of an evaluation to look backward, good evaluations also always look forward. They should not only record what happened in the past but also identify new questions and new areas of growth that could be addressed in the future. The evaluation isn't a bookend so much as a bridge. While it can serve to give closure to a field experience, it should always have an eye on linking learning from the field experience to where the student is headed next. How can the discoveries made at this site be furthered as the student leaves? How can questions be pursued? What is the next step? Evaluations are fodder for future learning contracts.

The benefit of a good evaluation is not always immediate. When evaluations are reread several months or even years out, sometimes the information within them makes even more sense and offers even more possibilities for reflection. With some hindsight and the benefit of ongoing feedback from course work and further ministry experience, the student is able to see patterns of thought and behavior that weren't always evident at the moment the evaluation was received. The evaluation becomes an important piece of a much larger puzzle in which the student continues to get a clearer picture of himself as a minister and as a person. Students should be encouraged to keep copies of their field education evaluations in their own personal files even after the official field education course is over. Solid, well-written evaluations are "gifts that keep giving."

Summary: A Structure for Life

The structure of discernment, preparation, self-assessment, setting learning goals, and evaluation—complemented by ongoing theological reflection—provides a way to order field education course work and ensure a high-quality learning experience. The purpose of introducing this structure, however, is not limited to formal ministry formation. It is a pattern intended for one's entire ministerial life.

When I first met the priest who was to serve as my field education director in graduate school, he told me that he had been in supervision for twenty years and was just about to write himself another new learning contract. I was a little worried about this. Who needs to be in supervision for twenty years? Isn't there a time when one's learning is complete? The answer, of course, is no. Having served as a field educator now for several years, it is increasingly clear to me how much remains to be learned, how many skills could use sharpening, how many incidents could bear further reflection. As long as there is room for growth, learning contracts, evaluations, and the other structures of field education will continue to be valuable. Field education allows students to become acquainted with a pattern of learning that can be used to structure their ongoing growth in ministry even after the formal paperwork is no longer required. Hopefully by the end of their field education sequence, the practices of discernment, self-assessment, creating learning goals, theological reflection, and evaluation will be, to use the language of Thomas Aquinas, *habitus*: a chosen way of life that becomes almost second nature.

Special Considerations for Off-Site Supervisors

If you are an off-site supervisor, you have probably recognized already that much of what is discussed in this chapter will need adaptation to fit your special circumstances. In some ways, your work will be simplified. For example, you will not have to prepare the site to receive the student. But in other ways, your work will be a little more challenging: It will be harder for you to know what kinds of possibilities exist at the site to help the student meet his learning objectives. Also, you will not have as many opportunities to actually see the student in ministry, and so you will have less personal observation on which to write the evaluation.

There are two ways in which these disadvantages can be minimized. The first is to visit the student on-site at least once during the placement. Have the student give you a tour, meet with her coworkers, be present at the class that she is teaching or the communion call she is making. This will give you a stronger sense of the student in ministry. The second possibility is to build some sort of relationship with an on-site liaison whom you and the student can call together if questions exist during the placement, especially when establishing what sorts of activities will be included in the learning contract. If appropriate, this on-site liaison could also be asked to meet with the student toward the end of the semester to offer feedback that could inform the evaluation process.

The good news is that, chances are, you will have few problems. Students are generally approved for off-site supervision only if they are already employed at the site, in which case they know the site and the ministry well, or if the field education program director feels they are energetic and mature enough to handle the extra legwork required on their part to negotiate a more complicated field education arrangement. While off-site supervision has challenges, it is approved only when it appears that the advantages will significantly outweigh the disadvantages. It makes possible wonderful placements that otherwise would not have been viable. After the placement is over, students and supervisors who go this route often agree that on-site supervision would be desirable, but their experience was still so valuable they have no regrets about the choice they made.

Questions for Reflection and Discussion

1. What would be good clues to you about whether to take on a field education student at this time? What kinds of indicators in yourself or in the student would let you know that a particular match would not be a good one?
2. What preparation would need to take place at your site before a student's arrival? What kind of orientation of the student, staff, and community would be needed?
3. What kind of opportunities would exist at your site for a student who came to you wanting to:

- work on overcoming a fear of public speaking?
- overcome racist patterns of thought or behavior?
- work on developing better leadership skills?
- learn how to build community?
- discover whether a history of alcoholism was impacting her capacity for ministry?
- build better relational skills with women or men?

4. For each of the possibilities mentioned in #3 above, what kind of strategies might become part of the student's learning contract? What kind of measurements would you suggest to know whether progress was being made?

5. What part of the evaluation process, if any, do you find most personally challenging? How comfortable do you feel offering positive feedback to another? How comfortable do you feel offering constructive criticism to another? How comfortable do you feel with the authority entrusted to you as a supervisor?

CHAPTER 2 NOTE

1. Sean P. Reynolds, *Multiply the Ministry: A Practical Guide for Grassroots Ministry Empowerment* (Winona, MN: St. Mary's Press, 2001), 25.

Theological Reflection: The Heart of Field Education

In the last chapter, we outlined the fivefold structure that undergirds ministerial field education: selection of the match, preparation of the environment, the learning contract, the evaluation, and theological reflection. While the first four of these could be addressed in the pages following the outline, the last is so substantive that it merits at minimum a chapter of its own.

The term *theological reflection* is a buzzword in contemporary Christian circles. The *Program of Priestly Formation* argues that theological reflection is a necessary part of the seminarian's pastoral formation as a way to integrate the future pastor's theological learning with the experiences he faces in day-to-day parish life.[1] *Co-Workers in the Vineyard*, the USCCB's document on the formation of lay ecclesial ministers, advocates for theological reflection as a spiritual practice to form mature, faith-filled ministers of the Church.[2] Hospitals, schools, and parishes sprinkle the language of theological reflection throughout mission statements and board meetings and lift up the tool as essential in the formation of future institutional leaders. When communities of faith face difficult decisions about the future, they often claim that more theological reflection is needed. But what is theological reflection? How can one practice address so many needs?

In the broadest sense, theological reflection refers to any process that helps persons make connections between their life and their faith. Moral theologian Richard Gula defines Christian theological reflection as a conscious effort "both to interpret life's experiences in light of God's purposes in Jesus and to understand the Christian story about God in the light of what we are experiencing day to day."[3] The practice rests on two central convictions. The first conviction is that experience can be revelatory. In the Catholic tradition, the world in which we live is not perceived as being inherently evil or separate from God. Rather, God loves the world and chooses to make Godself known through it. When we reflect on our own experience and on the cumulative experience of our profession, our culture, and our Church, there is wisdom to be found. Indeed, God is to be found there. To use language more familiar to many Catholics, we could say that experience has the potential to be sacramental—to mediate for us an experience of God. Without this conviction that human experience is innately sacred, taking the time to seek connections between God's plan and our lives makes little sense.

The second conviction upon which theological reflection rests builds on the first. It is the conviction that our faith life and daily life are not meant to be two separate spheres but one. In our society we hear often of the "Sunday Christian" or sometimes even the "Christmas and Easter Christian"—the person who professes belief on one day of the week or year but lives as though it has no impact on his life all of the other days. Sometimes language within our faith tradition about what is considered "sacred" and what is considered "secular" encourages this divide, as does common cultural use of phrases like "separation of church and state" or "public versus private." I am not arguing that these distinctions are not helpful or often necessary, but rather that, loosely thrown about in our conversation, they contribute to a bifurcation in the American mind between what belongs to the realm of God and what does not. The practice of theological reflection is based on the belief that there should be an intimate connection between what we say we believe and what we do. In theological language, we might rephrase this to claim that there should be a harmony between our "professed theology" and our "operative theology."

While all those who speak and write about theological reflection share these convictions about the potential for and value of making connection between faith and life, it is important to note that they will advocate making these connections for many different reasons: more educated pastoral praxis; a deeper spiritual life; the desire to ensure the Christian identity of an institution; pastoral planning; formation of small Christian communities; or a myriad of other possibilities. In each case, the process that we design to make connections between God's story and our story is going to be shaped by the outcome that we hope to attain in the end. Different reflective questions will be asked based on the reason why the reflection is being done. A theological reflection process designed to help small Christian communities relate the Sunday readings to their lives will look a little different from the process a parish council uses to establish a five-year pastoral plan or a chaplaincy student uses as part of clinical pastoral education. In this chapter, we will limit our focus to approaches toward theological reflection that best serve the formation of a minister within the context of field education, aware that there are many other reasons why persons reflect and, hence, many approaches beyond those addressed here.

Theological Reflection Within Ministerial Field Education

Theological reflection, as noted in chapter 1, is to be a constitutive element of all ministerial field education programs. Alongside the experience of actually doing ministry, it is considered the primary educational method of the discipline of field education. Probably about 50 percent of the learning that takes place during a placement happens in the ministry itself, and about 50 percent happens in the conscious reflection upon that ministry. Theological reflection in field education can happen in a variety of forums. Some field education programs have students meet regularly with other field education students and an instructor to do theological reflection while they are in their placements. Some require that students form "lay committees" at their placement site to do theological reflection. (More will be said about these committees at the end of this chapter.) Almost all require that students meet with their supervisor for reflection. The timing of these reflection sessions varies. Some will ask that students and their supervisors meet weekly, some every other week, some once a month. Regardless of the spacing of these sessions, they are extremely important to the success of the placement. If at all possible, students and supervisors should mark dates for theological reflection on their calendars at the beginning of the placement to make sure that the meetings receive priority in the midst of busy schedules.

Each supervisory theological reflection session should be at least an hour in length and preferably seventy-five minutes. Early on in the placement students and supervisors should decide how the agenda will be set for each meeting. As a general principle, students choose an incident or a theme from their ministry experience to bring to theological reflection, but sometimes it may be appropriate for the supervisor to ask the student to reflect on an aspect of the student's ministry that the supervisor believes merits reflection. In the beginning, students may have a hard time finding material for theological reflection. Theological reflection can be done on any experience, but often it is easiest to start with a problem that demands a response or an event that evokes strong emotion. The challenge, for better or for worse, is that in the beginning of a placement, there frequently is no such problem or event. Students may need help discovering how ordinary ministry encounters can still be rich fodder for reflection. It is also possible to have students reflect on patterns or themes that they are seeing in their ministry. Several small incidents with a common theme can be a great starting place for theological reflection.

One of the great temptations of the supervisory meeting is to turn it into a small business meeting rather than a theological reflection (TR) session. Students and supervisors can end up having a casual chat about how things are going on-site or taking care of organizational matters during their reflection time. Such detail-oriented meetings do need to happen, but they should be scheduled for a time other than the theological reflection session. TR sessions should focus on a single incident or theme, and the nature of the meeting should be reflective, not problem-solving or planning.

Another occasional temptation of TR sessions is that they can become therapy or spiritual direction in disguise. In the course of theological reflection, students often become more deeply aware of how their personal life is impacting their ministry. They also, hopefully, become more aware of how their image of God and relationship with God are affected by and affecting their ministry. The difference between therapy or spiritual direction and theological reflection, however, is one of both focus and forum. In theological reflection during field education, the primary focus is on the "self as minister" versus the "self as self" or the "self as child of God."

It is a question of nuance. More importantly, therapy and spiritual direction both belong to what is sometimes called in ecclesial circles "internal forum" versus "external forum." In situations of internal forum, the primary allegiance of the professional is to the person she is serving. For example, the therapist's first duty is to the client. Therapists are expected to maintain strict confidentiality regarding what the client reveals to them. The same holds for the spiritual director. The directee should feel comfortable speaking freely about whatever he wants to reveal to the director. The supervisory relationship, however, is one of external forum. The supervisor is definitely in a role of service to the student but as a means of serving the larger Church. While ordinarily these two allegiances are not in conflict, if a tension between the two did occur, the supervisor's ultimate loyalty has to be to the Church. If the supervisor has concerns about a student's suitability for ministry, that concern cannot remain confidential but needs to be shared with the director of the student's ministry program. In chapter 4, the question of boundaries in supervision will be discussed at greater length. For now, however, know that most of the time these temptations can be easily skirted if the student and supervisor take time to prepare for the session in advance.

Preparing for a Theological Reflection Session

Many supervisors find it helpful to have students write down the event (or short pattern of events) that they hope to reflect upon. Some even request that the student hand in the written narration a day or so in advance to give the supervisor time to think about the incident and jot down a few questions before meeting the student. The opportunity to prepare questions often results in richer reflection experiences. Writing down the incident can also help the student sharpen her memory of the experience and narrow her focus before formal reflection begins. It can help put parameters around what is to be reflected upon so that the narration of the event alone doesn't compose half of the reflection session.

Sometimes students find it helpful to write out their events verbatim, which means that they transcribe a record of the dialogue that took place as accurately as they can. Other times students may find it helpful just to narrate the event or theme. Narrations should generally be one typed page or less and free of judgments and assumptions. When narrating an event for reflection, it is important to ascertain who, what, when, and how, but not why. We short-circuit the reflection process by interpreting too early why an event took place or why people acted as they did. This disallows other possible interpretations to surface as part of the reflection. One way to help students arrive at a more objective narration is to have them reread what they have written and draw a line through the "because" statements—both literal and implied—in their writing. Sometimes students think that this means they are also supposed to scratch their feelings from their narration. Not true. Their own feelings are very much part of the facts of the case, but they should be careful not to ascribe feelings or motivations to *another* unless the other person articulated them.

Opening the Theological Reflection Session

At the start of a theological reflection, it is good to open with a moment of centering silence and prayer, asking God to draw near during this time of reflection. A sample opening prayer is given on the next page, but you may find spontaneous prayer works best.

Prayer for Opening Theological Reflection

Gracious God, we thank you for calling us into ministry here
at (*name of ministry site*).
We thank you for the people whom we meet here,
for the sacredness of the space, for the joy of the work
itself.
We thank you for being alive and active here
and for the ways in which you continue to shape and mold
us through all that takes place here.
We ask you to draw near to us in a special way now
as we bring forward one small slice of this ministry to ponder in a deeper way.
Open our eyes to see what it is that you want us to see in
this event.
Open our ears that we may hear what it is you would have
us to hear.
Open our minds to new thoughts and understandings.
Open our hearts that through this reflection we may arrive
at a deeper love of you and your people.
May this time help us to become ever more fully the minis-
ters that you dream us to be.
We ask this in the name of your son, Jesus Christ, and in the
power of the Spirit.
Amen.

After praying, ask the student to narrate the event or theme that he wants to reflect upon. Even if a written narration has been prepared in advance, there is something valuable about having the student read it aloud. Sometimes new nuances become apparent that are not ascertained in reading alone. Afterward, take a moment to ask clarifying questions about any part of the event that is unclear. This is not the time to ask probing or leading questions (e.g., "Why did you do that?" or "Do you think that . . . ?") but only to ask information-oriented questions concerning pieces of the narration that seem fuzzy or incomplete.

Questions of Analysis

Now begins the reflection in earnest. The first reflective question to be asked in almost every theological reflection is the "What happened?" question. No event happens in a vacuum. Sometimes we think of events like isolated stars in the sky—pinpricks of light floating in a dark void. When we draw constellations, we perceive ourselves to be "connecting the dots." In theological reflection, it can be helpful to reverse the image. What if, in truth, there exist invisible lines crisscrossing the sky, and where they intersect a star occurs? The first task of theological reflection in field education is to try to identify all of the "invisible lines" that crisscrossed to give rise to this particular event appearing in concrete time and space. There are three main "lines" that we want to make certain we ask about every time we analyze an event:

the line of faith tradition

the line of culture

the line of personal experience

When we look for the **line of faith tradition**, we are looking for all of the ways in which our Christian heritage—including interpretation of scripture, worship practices, Church teaching and law, Church history and politics, and contemporary ecclesial trends—has given rise to the event's emergence. For instance, we need to ask, "How does the Church's teaching on *(the particular topic)* affect the situation?" "How has the charism of the institution's founding religious order affected this event's history?" "What role does the structure of the Church play in this situation's existing as it does?"

When we look for the **line of culture**, we are asking about the myriad ways that our cultural history and context have played a role in the event's emergence. We ask questions about trends in American history and current events while also looking at the role more specific ethnic histories play. For example, "How does the Germanic (African, Irish, Latino, etc.) heritage of this community play a role?" When looking at the line of culture, we also want to ask questions about worldview: "What is the relationship to time that is evident in this event?" "What is the relationship to the land, to material goods, to the human body, to the human community?" We must also examine what philosophical frames of mind are operative: Utilitarianism? Pragmatism? Nihilism?

When we look for the **line of personal experience**, we are looking for ways in which our personal life histories, including family histories, have played a role in the situation's existing as it does, and moreover, how they have played a role in our interpretation of the event. This line of questioning can be very personal and, hence, quite sensitive. It includes asking questions like, "How does your family's way of dealing with conflict affect how you responded to this conflict?" "How does your longtime friendship with this parishioner play a role in what happened?" But it also includes asking, "Does your longtime friendship with this parishioner affect how you are looking at this situation now?" "Is there any-thing in your life history that predisposes you to have a bias toward one side or the other as we reflect on this?" It is important that the supervisor also ask herself these kinds of questions to get in contact with any bias or interpretative lens that she brings to the reflection. Both parties need to be aware as much as possible of how their life histories impact how they hear an event—and each other.

Questions of Analysis

- What historical lines have crisscrossed for this event to emerge in time and space?
- What aspects of our faith tradition have been involved in giving birth to this event?
- What aspects of our culture have been involved in giving birth to this event?
- What aspects of the student's personal history have been involved in giving birth to this event?
- What aspects of both of our life histories impact how we hear and interpret this event now?

The goal of this kind of analysis is not to make judgments about the "goodness" or "badness" of the particular strands that have fed into the situation's existing as it does, but sim-ply to note that they have played a role. The value of such analysis is not always immediately felt. Sometimes naming the various lines that have intersected leads to no great new insight. The value is in naming these lines week after week.

If theological reflection is a regular practice, one will begin to see that some strands reappear repeatedly. For instance, a few years ago, when a group of field education students located in a diversity of ministry sites looked back over the theological reflections they had done during the course of the previous year, they discovered how frequently the themes of American individualism and hurriedness wove through all of their cases. They were working in prisons, parishes, domestic violence centers, archdiocesan offices, hospitals, and schools, but noted similar experiences across the board with these two very strong cultural themes. The pervasiveness of these themes became fodder for further reflection about how they wanted to respond to questions of time and interpersonal relationships in their own lives. In another instance, a student was able to see how her grief over a deceased sibling had come up as a strand in several situations. It was never the dominant issue in any one case but a subtle thread in a number of cases. When this was pointed out, she could see how a loss that she thought had healed long ago was continuing to impact her as a minister, and she chose to see a counselor.

Coming to the Heart of the Matter

Analysis of the incident is a critical step in the theological reflection process for field education students, but it is only the beginning. The next step is to allow the analysis to give rise to further questions. What are all of the questions that the case raises for the two of you? What does it make you wonder about? Write down whatever surfaces. Some of the questions will be questions about the characters in the narration: "I wonder why the bishop responded as he did." "Why does the DRE always insist on planning so far ahead?" "Why did the prisoner refuse to let me visit him again?" Only the persons involved can answer these questions, and it isn't very fruitful to continue reflecting on them without the other person's presence because it would only be conjecture.

Other questions will be factual in nature: "What did the bishop write about in his new pastoral letter?" "What steps need to be taken to plan for next year's religious education calendar?" "When will the prisoner be eligible for parole?" These questions can be addressed via research and aren't really reflective questions.

Other questions will surface, however, that are more general in nature or within the sphere of personal influence: "What does right relationship with the bishop look like?" "How should I address my tension with the DRE?" "Am I really called to this ministry if the prisoners don't want to see me? How do I know?" These kinds of questions hold great reflective potential.

After surfacing all possible questions, ask the student to choose one question that seems the most pressing for him. Which question seems to best capture the heart of the matter? This stage in the process is very important. Without some narrowing, the theological reflection process can get quite unwieldy and disjointed. Choosing only one core question will help give focus and depth to the remainder of the reflection. Know, however, that you can always return to the same incident at another time and reflect on it through the lens of a different question.

Coming to the Heart of the Matter

Having analyzed the case, what kinds of questions does the case raise for you?

Of all of these questions, which one question stands out? Which one question represents the heart of the matter for you?

Most of the time, you will discover that "heart of the matter" questions tend to fall into three categories: **Action** ("What am I to do?"), **Meaning** ("Where is the meaning in this for me?"), and **Identity** ("Who am I to be?"). Recall what we talked about earlier in the chapter regarding the various approaches that writers have taken toward theological reflection: different desired outcomes will require different sets of reflective questions. A case about an event that beckons a decision and course of action is different from one about an event that took place some time ago but still haunts the student, continuing to evoke strong feelings. As the facilitator of the theological reflection, it can be good to have a couple of different reflection strategies in your supervisory "tool belt" so that you can adapt your facilitation to best suit the kind of "heart of the matter" question the student is asking. "One size fits all" theological reflection doesn't really exist. On the following pages, we will look at a couple of different strategies for reflecting on different sorts of questions.

Questions of Action

"What am I to do?" is perhaps the most common "heart of the matter" raised in ministerial theological reflection. Perhaps the student is having trouble with one of the children in her second grade religious education class. Perhaps he isn't quite sure whether to try to bring feuding members of an RCIA team together to talk or to just let things ride. Perhaps she is questioning whether to take part in a controversial protest or not. In all of these situations and innumerable more, the student is being asked to make a decision and needs theological reflection to make sure that the decision is well informed, on target, and in line with his deepest values. The student wants his action to be a conscious response rather than simply a reaction.

In 1980, James and Evelyn Whitehead published the book *Method in Ministry* precisely to address the kinds of "action-oriented" questions that ministers and their communities face every day. An early book in the literature about theological reflection, *Method in Ministry* is also regarded as a classic in the field—commonly footnoted in other texts about TR. The Whiteheads outline what they call both a "model" and a "method" of theological reflection, akin to identifying the core players in a dialogue and then how their conversation moves in time and space. The three critical dialogue partners that they establish in their model are those that we have named earlier in our questions of analysis: experience, tradition, and culture.[4] They recognize that each of these voices not only plays a role in making the situation as it is, but that each voice also possesses a wisdom that can be drawn upon in working toward a solution. Often in our personal decision making, we have a voice that we bias to the exclusion of other voices, and we even bias certain strands within that one voice. We react in a certain way because "it's just common sense," unaware that "common sense" is frequently culture masquerading itself as the only norm. We defend ourselves, saying, "This is the way that we've always done it," mistaking personal experience of how it has always been done for the totality of experience. We argue, "This is Church teaching," while standing on a very small fragment of the Church's tradition. This kind of decision making is analogous to standing on one leg in an earthquake. In ministry, the Whiteheads acknowledge, the ground is constantly moving beneath our feet. We stand the best chance of remaining upright if we have more than one "leg" to stand on and if these legs "have knees." That is, if they are able to bend, absorb, and balance each other out.

The **first stage** in the Whitehead theological reflection method is what they call "**attending**." This means listening to what the voices of tradition, culture, and personal experience have to share about the heart of the matter. What wisdom does each have to bear concerning the issue at hand? When asking this question, we should try to stretch the range of sources that we normally rely upon. For example, in the area of tradition, we should certainly consider what wisdom scripture might hold on the topic, but we should also look to Church history, canon law, magisterial teaching, liturgical documents, lives of the saints, the writings of theologians, etc. In the realm of culture, we are looking for more than a bland, generic stereotype of what "American culture" might say about a topic. We want to ask about the wisdom of sociology, psychology, organizational development, and anthropology. How does law treat this issue? What about the media? Do you see any connections to literature, music, or art? Would the various ethnicities within the United States perceive the issue differently? Listening to personal experience includes listening to what we have learned from our own personal life histories about the best way to address a situation. It includes listening to the stories of our families and communities that we value. What wisdom do they have to contribute? How would they have us respond?

Like the stage of analysis that we discussed previously, the purpose of attending is not to make judgments among the voices, but simply to "put them all out on the table." Attending helps us become aware of the breadth of knowledge and wisdom that can be drawn upon and the many possible responses that exist.

The **second stage** of the Whitehead process, however, brings these voices into actual conversation with one another, acknowledging that sometimes the voices are in harmony, but sometimes they actually contradict. The Whiteheads call this stage the **"crucible of assertion,"** highlighting the sometimes painfully cacophonous nature of the conversation as varying opinions and impressions slide toward the narrow end of the funnel together and compete to emerge in first place. At this stage in the process we must ask, "Of all that we have heard from the various voices, what is most valuable to listen to in this situation? Are there ways in which certain voices harmonize here, leading to a clear sense of direction? Are there voices that are in conflict? Which one will you side with and why? How do you judge among these voices and on what grounds?"

The **final stage** of the Whitehead process moves **toward action**. Theological reflection, from their perspective, results in more intentional behavior on the part of the reflection participants. The concluding questions in the process can include more general considerations: "What is the Church called to do regarding this situation? What change is needed in our culture concerning this issue?" But at some point it must always move to a personal level: "How do you think *you* are called to respond to this issue?" And it must also move toward concreteness: "What is one step that you could take within this next week toward that outcome?" Making the step concrete is very important. It keeps the reflection from ending with grand platitudes and ethereal plans such as, "I will become a friendlier person" or "I need to become more involved in the civic life of the community." It also names something to which the student is willing to be held accountable, such as "I will stay after Masses to greet people this Sunday" or "I will write a letter to the alderman about the dangerous conditions of the school crossing this week." Sometimes the answer to "What should I do?" ends up being "I need to get more information about . . ." or "I need to think more about . . ." These are fine action statements as long as they include concrete plans as to how that information will be gathered or when continued pondering will be done. Sometimes the answer to "What should I do?" may even end up being "Nothing." That is okay, too. Sometimes doing nothing produces the greatest change of all.

Questions of Action

- What wisdom does your faith tradition have to contribute toward a pastoral response to the event?
- What wisdom could the resources of culture (the social sciences, literature, art, etc.) bring to bear?
- What wisdom do you bring from your personal experience that could be helpful to remember?
- How do you discern among these voices to find which information is most valuable to you in your pastoral decision making?
- What is the most desirable outcome in this situation? What is one step that you could take this week toward that outcome?

Questions of Meaning

As noted earlier, many cases that students bring forward revolve around what is the best way to handle an emerging situation or involve looking back at a situation that just happened and ascertaining the best way of dealing with similar situations that may occur in the future. For these kinds of cases, a Whitehead approach to theological reflection works particularly well. But sometimes, we encounter cases in which there is nothing to be done, cases that stand out in their singularity and seem unlikely to repeat themselves, cases about which the student continues to have strong emotions or lingering questions. Perhaps a student has had an amazing last conversation with a person on his deathbed. Perhaps the student receives a meaningful thank-you card from a teen in the youth group who seemed particularly hard to reach. Perhaps a retreat that took months to plan is now over, and the student feels very "flat." There are *kairos* moments of grace or, in some cases, dis-grace, that have a symbolic quality to them. It is as if these moments or events have something to say to us even after they are long past. In some cases, we could still ask of these situations, "How should I respond? Is there anything I should do?" But the heart of the matter seems to be more, "What does this mean? What is God trying to say to me?"

A good clue to the supervisor that the reflection should be angled toward this direction is when emotion plays a central role in the student's writing or vocalization of the event. Sometimes the student will make it easy by stating outright, "I felt so angry" or "I still get a chill down my spine." But, often, he will give only subtle hints through his posture or tone of voice. And then you can test your intuition by asking. For example, check out your perceptions by asking, "I am wondering—do you feel any sadness about this event?" It is always okay to guess and be wrong. Asking may actually help the student to articulate more clearly what feelings are latent in the narration ("No, I am really more frustrated"). If you discover that the heart of the matter in a case is more a question of meaning, you may want to structure the remainder of your reflection time together in another way.

In their book, *The Art of Theological Reflection*, Patricia O'Connell Killen and John de Beer wrestle with the question of how persons come to find meaning and insight through the events of their lives. Out of their experience of working with multiple faith-based groups over numerous years, they discovered that there is a natural, predictable pattern to how the human mind moves toward insight.[5] First, they argue, in entering into an experience, a person will encounter feelings. If the person pays attention to those feelings, images will begin to arise. If the person considers and questions those images, the images will spark new insights and meaning. Insights lead the person to act differently. What can make this pattern of reflection "theological reflection," they note, is if faith is consistently drawn upon as a voice in the consideration and questioning of one's images. From here, they outline a way in which theological reflection can consciously mirror the natural reflection process.

The **first step** in a Killen and de Beer approach would be to **help the student come more deeply in contact with his feelings** undergirding the particular event. Sometimes, as noted earlier, the feelings are strong and simple, but more often the feelings are complex, multiple, and even muted: "I kind of feel angry, but I know that I shouldn't, so then I also feel disappointed in myself" or "I know I should feel glad, and I do, but I also feel a little nervous and overwhelmed." It is good to try to get all of the feelings out on the table, not only those that we feel most comfortable admitting. Students with a heavy bent toward the intellectual life can have a hard time becoming aware of feelings. When you ask how they feel about an incident, they may begin to respond, "I feel that . . ." This is simply a way of couching thought in the language of feeling. You will need to help them take the "that" out of their sentences. One helpful strategy can be to ask the student what is going on in her body as she recalls this event. Getting in touch with physical sensations in the body can give a good clue as to what is going on emotionally.

I remember a supervisory appointment as a student when I was describing a very difficult financial situation that threatened to mandate the end of my field placement in favor of a summer job. I continued to verbalize that I knew "God was in charge" and that "everything was going to turn out just fine" when my supervisor asked me to pay attention to my body posture. As I talked, I had slouched lower and lower in the chair. He said, "Your words are saying that you are just fine, but your body is saying that you have the weight of the world on your shoulders." This was immensely valuable feedback, making me more aware of my true emotions.

The **second step** in Killen and de Beer's approach is to **surface images** evoked by the feelings. Often in the process of describing feelings, students naturally express images that capture their feelings. For example, the student might say, "I felt like I was trapped in the spin cycle of a washing machine" or "It's like I'm on a roller coaster." Other times, it can be helpful to consciously feed back possible images, as my supervisor did for me. No image should be considered too ridiculous or mundane. It is okay to surface several and then to ask the student, "Which image best captures for you the dynamics of the situation as you see it?" or "Which image best captures the range of emotions you feel when you recall this event?"

Now, work further with the image, considering it from different views and asking creative questions of it. Killen and de Beer encourage asking first what life is like "within" the image. For example, what is life like when you "have the weight of the world on your shoulders" or when you "are on a roller coaster"? They encourage asking about what is life giving or hopeful about life in this image, as well as what is life draining: "What is the best thing about life when you are stuck in the spin cycle of a washing machine? What is the worst? What would be your greatest hope?"

Then, Killen and de Beer suggest juxtaposing life within the image with other voices, at least one of which is from the Christian tradition, perhaps using the following questions:

What Bible story surfaces in your mind in connection with your image? (It can be a direct connection or quite a loose one.) How would Christ or other characters in your story understand your image? What would they want to say to you about your image to help you understand it further? What is similar between your image and this scripture? What is different? What does our culture say to you about life within this image? Is its message the same as scripture's, or is it different? Is it in harmony with your own ideas or jarring?

Obviously, asking questions such as these requires a level of imagination that can feel a little awkward and even silly for adults. Killen and de Beer's method is definitely much more playful than other methods, as if it engages a different part of the brain. Some students might initially rebel against being asked, "What is your greatest hope when you are walking through three feet of syrup?" But, if they are willing to allow imagination into their theologizing, it sometimes yields surprising results. One of the gifts of this approach within a Catholic ministerial formation program is that it can help strengthen the student's overall capacity for "sacramental imagination"—the capacity to read and engage symbols.

The **final step** in a Killen and de Beer process is to **name the fruits of the reflection** as much as one is able and return to the original event by asking questions such as these: Is there any new insight that you gain from your pondering of these questions? Is there any insight that sheds new light on the experience you narrated in opening this reflection? How is your interpretation of your experience different for having spent this time reflecting upon it? Like the Whiteheads, Killen and de Beer emphasize that theological reflection should always result in action. They note that, if we are willing, insight naturally leads to action, but they also acknowledge that insight doesn't automatically mean behavior changes. As the proverb recalls, "The road to hell is paved with good intentions." They urge intentional prayer, planning, and asking support from other people as ways of ensuring that the insights gleaned in theological reflection continue to move forward in daily life.

Questions of Meaning

What feelings do you have in your body as you describe this event?

If you had to capture the dynamics of this situation in a picture or an image, what would it be?

What is life like when you are "inside" this image? What is hard (challenging/dangerous) about being within this image? Where is there hope in being within this image? What is lifegiving about being within the image?

What scripture passage (or other faith story) comes to mind when you consider this image? What would this passage have to say to your image? What does your image have to say to this passage?

What new insight into your original experience do you gain from your work with this image?

Is there any new behavior that you want to adopt out of this reflection?

Questions of Identity

Theological reflections that center around the question of identity are undoubtedly the most challenging to facilitate, because they ask for a greater amount of trust and vulnerability on the part of the student. When asking questions about what to do or what something means, students have the option to stand a short distance from what is being considered—it is something other than themselves. But when the heart of the matter is identity, the student's very understanding of herself *is* the focus of reflection. Fortunately, this kind of question does not often arise early in a placement, allowing time for trust in the supervisory relationship to develop first. It takes a certain level of self-awareness on the part of the student to be aware that one's sense of identity is playing a role in a case at all.

Two kinds of experiences tend to trigger questions about identity in field placements. One is the experience of some sort of failure or perceived failure. In some way the student's ministry is rejected or questioned. Perhaps attendance at the Bible study he organizes has dwindled to but one or two people. Perhaps a preaching elicits only yawns from the congregation. Perhaps the parent of a youth group member is upset about a decision that she has made. The student wonders both at a personal level ("Am I a bad person?" "Am I not as likeable as I thought I was?") and also at a professional level ("Am I not as competent as I thought I was?" "Is this really my call?").

The other triggering experience is one in which the student is accorded a new level of authority or expectation in the community for which he feels unready. Perhaps people come to him with questions he can't answer or bare their souls with revelations of their personal life that overwhelm him. Perhaps people who were friends before are now treating him differently, as if on a pedestal. The student wonders, "Who am I supposed to be?" "Can I be what people want me to be?" "What kind of relationship will I as a minister have with others?"

Both the Whitehead and Killen and de Beer approaches to theological reflection described earlier could be adapted to work with questions of identity. If you have found that one pattern or another has consistently worked well for the two of you in the past, you may want to continue to reflect in that direction. For example, you could ask the student to come up with a symbol that represents how she understands herself as a minister and have her dialogue with that symbol. It may be helpful, however, to pursue a line of reflection suggested by Kenneth Pohly in his book *Transforming the Rough Places: The Ministry of Supervision*.Pohly argues that "identity formation" is one of the most critical tasks of ministry supervision and one that is frequently undervalued in favor of skill development or problem solving.[6] Spending time in theological reflection on cases that raise the issue is one of the most effective ways of addressing this overall goal in field education.

Pohly considers the field education experience as a whole to be an "emerging story" in which the student's personal story and sense of self are continually engaging the community's story and sense of self. The particular lived experience that the student brings for reflection is one small part of that emerging story but can serve as a window into the overall emerging story. Theological reflection can help the student grow in awareness of how aspects of his own story—especially his ideas of who the minister is supposed to be—are influencing how he functions in the community, as well as helping the student become aware of how the community's story and understanding of him are being revealed in his experiences. This requires paying very close attention to the relating of the ministry incident itself and then helping the student "enlarge the story." This raises to a conscious articulation the values and convictions that undergird the student's behavior as a minister in a situation and affect the way that he tells the story. Enlarging the story helps the student evaluate what is included in the telling of the story and what she leaves out. Pohly argues that part of the work of the supervisor in theological reflection is to help the student paint a continually more honest and realistic portrait of the self in ministry.

When the heart of the matter is a question of identity, Pohly's **first step** would be to **take deeper the analysis that began the reflection time**, asking further questions about how one's sense of identity shaped the incident being reflected upon, as well as how the community's sense of identity had an influence. When focusing on developing the student's ministerial identity, the supervisor might want to ask questions such as:

- What model of ministry most influences the student's understanding of herself as a minister in this situation?
- Where does that model come from? Childhood mentors? Images from the tradition or culture?
- What are the beliefs and convictions that undergird her approach to ministry in this situation?
- What model of ministry most influences the community's understanding? Where does the community's model come from?

- What other models of ministering exist with the tradition that could have been drawn upon?
- What strengths and weaknesses does the student bring to living out her model of ministry?
- What are the strengths and weaknesses of the ministry model itself? In what situations does it serve her well?
- When does it seem to fall short? How could it be strengthened or enriched by other perspectives?

Occasionally, as noted earlier, the student's question about identity is more personal than professional. The experience of ministry can rattle not only our sense of self as minister, but also those things that we like to believe about ourselves as persons. Each of us would like to believe that we are competent, good, and worthy of love. We can tend to fall into an "all-or-nothing" mentality: Either I am competent or I am incompetent. I am good or I am evil. I am worthy or I am worthless. A mature personal identity recognizes that no one is totally competent, good, or worthy. We are all mixed bags. But that doesn't make us incompetent, evil, and worthless.[7] Questions to help a student explore personal identity might include:

- How does the student want to think of herself?
- How does she want to be perceived?
- How does the community think of itself?
- How would it like to be perceived?
- Where do these senses of self come from?
- Are there other ways of understanding ourselves from tradition or culture that we should be paying attention to?
- Is either the student's or the community's sense of self challenged or reaffirmed in any way by the event?

An important **second step** in Pohly's process is **checking for self-deception**. Since the supervisor's job is to help the student paint a realistic picture, she'll offer feedback such as, "You say that it's important to you that all of the groups in the parish feel like they have equal access to you. How possible is that?" or "You would like your clients here to consider you a friend. What does that mean to you? How are they like friends, and how are they not?" or "You say that it is not important what the kids say behind your back. Are you being honest with yourself?" These kinds of questions can help bring to light incongruities in the student's professed theology of ministry and his operative theology. They can also help surface unrealistic expectations of the minister.

Pohly's reflection **then moves toward "autobiographing" the story**—having the students practice telling the story of who they are as ministers and who they want to be as honestly as they can. He compares autobiographing to composing one's own music rather than playing another's music. It forces the students to articulate what they have learned about themselves as ministers and as persons and where they hope their learning leads. This stage could be guided by asking questions such as "If you had to say right now how you see yourself as a minister, what would you say?" "What kind of relationship do you want to have with the community you are serving in, and in particular the persons involved in this incident?" "Who do you hope to be in the future?"

Pohly's **last stage moves back toward the concrete**: "Is there anything further that you want to follow up on concerning the incident that you brought for reflection? **What are the next steps** that you want to take toward living out your vision of yourself as minister? How might your own life story change as a result of your choices?"

Questions of Identity

What vision of the minister/of the self is operative in your relating this incident? Where does that vision come from?

What vision of the minister/of the self is operative in the community in which you serve? Where does that vision come from?

Where are these visions in harmony? How do they challenge each other?

What other perspectives on this topic should we be listening to from our tradition and our culture?

Is there anything in the story we tell about ourselves that we should question? Any incongruities that we should explore further?

If you had to say whom you see yourself to be as a person/minister after this reflection, how would you articulate it?

Is there anything that you want to do as a result of this reflection?

Concluding the Theological Reflection Session

Just as it is good to begin a theological reflection session with prayer, it is good to end with prayer, too. Thank God together for the insights of the reflection and for the opportunity to grow in this way. Ask God's continued blessing on the ministry, and petition for the courage and perseverance needed to make good on the intentions for action and change stated during the reflection.

It can also be valuable to end with a short evaluation of the TR experience. How did the reflection go? What kinds of questions did the student find most helpful? Is there anything that you want to do differently in future sessions? Theological reflection tends to become richer the longer that a pair engages in the practice together. Over time, certain themes will begin to reappear, and connections will become evident where they were not before. Do not become discouraged if the conversation feels forced or awkward at first. Like two people learning to dance, after a while the two of you will no longer need to concentrate on what "step" comes next and will be able to enjoy the flow of the movement itself.

At the end of a TR session, it is important to either shred or place in a secure file any print copies of the student's narration in order to protect the privacy of the student and any other parties involved in the ministerial incident. If TR cases are kept during a student's placement, they should be destroyed at the end of the placement.

Summary

In this chapter, we have limited ourselves to approaches toward theological reflection that best serve the formation of a minister, but as we wrap up these thoughts, it is important to remember once again that the practice of theological reflection does not belong exclusively to ministers. Indeed, as Richard Gula argues, proficiency in theological reflection is the primary professional *duty* of the minister.[8] It is a skill learned first for oneself and one's own growth, but ultimately learned in order to be shared with others. As pastoral ministers, there is much in our job description that we share in common with other professionals—teachers, counselors, community organizers, etc.—but the one thing persons expect of ministers that they expect of no other is the capacity to help them make connections between their faith and their life.

Communities expect their ministers to be able to illumine these connections in their preaching and teaching, to ask about them in spiritual direction, to be guided by them in their administrative oversight. Communities also need to be empowered through the minister's facilitation and skill to find these connections for themselves, to be able to use their faith convictions to shape the decisions that they need to make together. Through the experience of doing theological reflection as part of field education, ministry students become more equipped to do the personal theological reflection integral to the spiritual and professional life of the minister, but also more equipped to eventually lead communities in doing the theological reflection integral to *their* growth and development as the People of God in service to the Reign of God.

An Added Note on the Potential of Lay Committees

Some ministry formation programs ask that their students begin to lead theological reflection in the community as part of the placement. This is not often the case in the student's first ministry placement, but it is a common requirement of students who are in advanced placements—a yearlong internship, for example. In these situations, students are generally asked to have a "lay committee." This is typically a group of four to seven people from the site who commit to meet together during the student's placement in their community. The purpose of a lay committee is to offer the student an inside glimpse of the site, helping him grasp the dynamics of the site and the issues important to the people there. They offer important feedback on the student's ministry from the perspective of the "person in the pew."

The student is responsible for calling the group together at regular intervals and for leading it in theological reflection on topics in which it would be valuable and appropriate to solicit the community's feedback. Sometimes, however, when the student is new to a site, it will fall to the supervisor to help find members who can be part of the student's lay committee. The supervisor will know much better than the student who might have the time and insight to be a good lay committee member. Committee members must be persons who will take the invitation to assist in a student's formation for ministry seriously. They should be persons who know the site and the people of the site well, but perhaps whose voices have not been regularly engaged in the leadership of the site. As much as possible they should be the "average Janes and Joes" of the community. Lay committees are most easily convened in congregational settings and may not even be viable in every field site, but they are a valuable way of helping the student to practice leading, not only participating in, communal theological reflection.

A SAMPLE INVITATION LETTER TO A POTENTIAL LAY COMMITTEE MEMBER

Dear [Name]:

An oft-quoted proverb says, "It takes a village to raise a child." Less well known, but equally true, is the ancient practice of our faith community: "It takes a Church to form a minister."

This fall, our *(parish/other)* community has been asked to help in the education and formation of a ministry intern from *(name of ministry institution)*.

(Intern's name) is a *(seminarian, lay minister, etc.)* completing *(his/her)* *(degree/certificate)* at *(name of ministry institution)*. *(S/he)* will be with us *(three months / nine months / one year)* as part of an internship. While here, *(s/he)* will *(offer a brief description of the intern's proposed ministry)*.

I will be mentoring *(intern's name)* while *(s/he)* is at *(site name)*. However, as part of *(intern's name)*'s internship, *(s/he)* is asked to reflect on *(his/her)* experience and receive feedback on *(his/her)* ministry from others in our community. I have been asked to convene a lay committee for *(intern's name)* that will meet with *(him/her)* *(number of)* times over the course of *(his/her)* internship, or approximately once every *(three/five/etc.)* weeks, for one-hour sessions. During these sessions, which will be led by *(intern's name)*, *(s/he)* will bring incidents from *(his/her)* ministry here that *(s/he)* would like to reflect upon and gather feedback from the people who know this community best. I consider you to be one of those persons.

I am asking whether you might be willing to serve on *(intern's name)*'s lay committee. I recognize that it is a significant time commitment, but I believe that you have real insight that could help *(intern's name)* get the most out of *(his/her)* time with our community this year. I believe that it is extremely important that our future ministers receive feedback from many voices in our Church, not only my voice or those in the academic setting.

If you are open to being part of *(intern's name)*'s education and willing to serve as a lay committee member, I ask you to give me a call *(phone number)* or e-mail me *(e-mail address)* before *(date)*, and we can speak about it more. I would like to give *(intern's name)* a list of four to seven persons who have agreed to serve on *(her/his)* lay committee by the beginning of the following week so that *(s/he)* might contact them to schedule the times and dates for the sessions. Thank you ever so much for considering this invitation.

Sincerely,
(Your name & title)

Questions for Reflection and Discussion

1. How did you understand theological reflection before reading this chapter? How has the process outlined in this chapter expanded or altered your understanding?
2. Is there anything missing from the process outlined that you would like to add? Are there other questions you think would be valuable to pursue with a student?
3. With which approach to theological reflection (Whitehead, Killen and de Beer, or Pohly) are you most familiar or comfortable? Which will you find more challenging to facilitate? Are there any you find uncomfortable? Are there other approaches with which you are more familiar?
4. What particular strengths do you bring to the theological reflection process? Theological education? Facility with scripture? Sharp cultural analysis? The wisdom of much life experience? Creative imagery? The ability to ask good questions?
5. What kinds of knowledge and skills would help you to become an even better reflection facilitator?

CHAPTER 3 NOTES

1. *PPF 5*, #239 and #248.
2. *CWV*, 42. Also mentioned later in the document as a tool for intellectual formation (p. 47) and pastoral formation (p. 50).
3. Gula, 54.
4. James D. and Evelyn Eaton Whitehead, *Method in Ministry: Theological Reflection and Christian Ministry*, rev. ed. (Kansas City: Sheed & Ward, 1995).
5. Patricia O'Connell Killen and John de Beer, *The Art of Theological Reflection* (New York: The Crossroad Publishing Company, 1994).
6. Kenneth Pohly, *Transforming the Rough Places: The Ministry of Supervision* (Franklin, TN: Providence House Publishers, 2001). See esp. pp. 151–175.
7. Douglas Stone, Bruce Patton, Sheila Heen. *Difficult Conversations: How to Discuss What Matters Most* (New York: Penguin Books, 1999), 112–121.
8. Gula, 54.

CHAPTER 4

Common Issues in Field Education

Perusing the section headings of this chapter might lead one to conclude that field education supervision can be a messy and complicated affair with many pitfalls to try to avoid. That is only half true. Field education supervision is about being in a relationship with another human, and that is always complicated, but the issues discussed in this chapter are not so much to be avoided as embraced as learning opportunities. At some point in ministry, everyone is going to have the opportunity to work with persons of other cultures, to be involved in conflict, to encounter a situation that begs confrontation, and everyone is going to endure a time crunch. If these things emerge in the course of a field placement—all the better! Field education can offer the opportunity to practice working through these challenges in a safe, learning-focused environment, an environment in which making some mistakes is still okay. Once someone is employed full time in ministry, the workplace environment may not be quite as hospitable to error.

Conflict

One of the best things that can happen during a field education placement is a good conflict—a genuine difference of view about something of significance. Many field education experiences proceed very smoothly, and no conflict between the student and the site or the student and the supervisor ever emerges. But, in just as many cases (if not more), the student and supervisor will hit some sort of "bump in the road." There are as many potential sources of conflict in field education as there are students. Sometimes the differences revolve around varied opinions—how to interpret a new ecclesial statement, how to handle a problem, etc. Most of the time, however, differences are rooted in varied expectations concerning the field placement: the supervisor thought the student would be better prepared; the student thought the supervisor would be more flexible about hours on-site; etc.

There exists the temptation to just brush the matter under the rug and pretend that either it isn't there or it isn't a big deal. But one of the best learning experiences in field education can be to practice bringing the matter out into the open for honest conversation. Many students have never had the opportunity to work through a conflict in a healthy, adult manner. Perhaps the conflicts they witnessed growing up frequently turned into yelling matches or even violence. Perhaps they resulted in permanently fractured relationships and long, uncomfortable periods of silence. Perhaps they have heard all of their lives that good Christians aren't ever angry or they don't argue with one another. They may have entered into a pattern of avoiding all forms of conflict, even necessary ones. Or they may have become used to solving problems by talking to other people rather than the ones with whom they are upset—a pattern called "triangulation." If they have the opportunity to work through a conflict appropriately in the midst of field education, and the experience is a good one, they may feel more comfortable entering into another conflict in the future and begin to establish a new pattern of behavior.

Before discussing how to handle conflicts that emerge in field education, it may be helpful to summarize a few principles *about* conflict in general.[1] First, conflict has always been part of our Christian history. There was never a time in the Church, from the earliest days of the Acts of the Apostles, when there was not conflict. We should not expect our lives to be exempt. In fact, if conflict is absent in our communities, it is more often a sign that something is seriously wrong than something is very right. People argue only about what they care about. If no one is arguing, it could be a bad sign. All of our experience, however, hasn't made conflict easy. It is still difficult and often painful.

Next, there is a difference between conflict resolution and conflict management. Conflict resolution is when all parties are able to resolve their differences and agree with one another about the next steps forward. Conflict management, on the other hand, means that the parties are able to live and work with one another while still disagreeing on the source of the conflict. While conflict resolution is always desirable, conflict management is often more realistic and shouldn't be undervalued. Lastly, while conflict that is neither resolved nor managed always damages the relationship, conflict that *is* resolved or managed actually leads to a stronger relationship—perhaps even stronger than if the conflict had never happened. Relationships are deepened and enriched by conflict done well.

Of course, articulating these truths and integrating them into our day-to-day choices are two very different things. In theory, we know conflict can be positive, but even as supervisors, it's not often a conviction we like to test-run. C.S. Lewis once offered the analogy of being handed a rope that promises to hold up to 125 pounds without snapping.[2] If someone asked us whether we believed the rope could do that, we'd say, "Sure." If the person followed by saying, "Well, here is your best friend, who weighs about 120 pounds. Let's tie the rope around the waist and let her down over the side of this cliff," we'd have new doubts. One of the things that can make us much more comfortable testing the promise of healthy conflict is familiarity with communication tools that have been utilized effectively by others. There are many excellent books and workshops on the topic of conflict resolution and management that you may wish to explore as a way of strengthening your skill in this critical area of supervision. As a way of summarizing some of the key points in the literature on conflict and confrontation, let us consider the following seven points.[3]

1. *Know that some things are worth bringing up; some things aren't.* Before raising a difficult issue with a student, consider your reasons for doing so. Good reasons for raising an issue include wanting to understand better the student's actions and reasoning, wanting to express your feelings and thinking, and the desire to problem-solve together. Inadequate reasons for raising an issue include wanting to persuade the student of the error of his ways, wanting to change the other's point of view, and wanting to give the other "a piece of your mind." Also, if you realize that the issue at hand is more your own personal issue than one that exists between you, it is not worth bringing up. It is always wise to reflect before bringing up an issue for discussion, to identify one's rationale and hopes for the conversation.

2. *Avoid triangulation.* Occasionally in supervision, another staff member (parishioner, client, etc.) may come to you

and ask you to address a matter with a student. Avoid confronting on behalf of another. Instead, encourage the other person to talk with the student directly. If direct confrontation fails, you can offer to help facilitate a conversation between the student and the other person, but both the student and the other person must be present. As a general rule of good leadership and Christian charity, whenever two persons are speaking negatively about a third, the third has a right to be there. Communication in field education should be as transparent and respectful as possible.

3. *Time it right.* If you decide to raise an issue of concern with a student, as a matter of justice, do it as soon as possible after the provoking incident. Do not hold it in the back of your mind to bring up at the time of evaluation. At the same time, don't try to have the conversation "off the cuff." Give yourself time to calm down if you have strong emotions and time to consider how to structure the conversation. When you bring up the issue, make sure that the two of you have adequate time to engage the topic. Don't try to bring it up in the hallway on the way to something or in the last five minutes of an appointment. If, in return, the student initiates a difficult conversation and catches you off guard, it is okay to acknowledge that what he has raised is important, and you want to talk about it but feel unprepared or hurried right now. In these cases, schedule a time to talk as soon as possible.

4. *Realize that conflict is always about more than the facts of an incident.* We often operate under the belief that if we just got all of "the facts" of a situation right, we would all agree. We desire to limit conversations to the realm of reason, not wanting to get bogged down in feelings and all the messy stuff of human relations. The truth is that the facts of a situation are rarely what the

disagreement is about. Both parties, for example, agree that the youth group was without an adult chaperone for a half hour of their gathering. What they disagree about is interpretation of the facts: whether this lack of supervision was important. And what makes the disagreement so difficult to talk about *is* the very range and depth of feelings that the parties possess: The supervisor feels angry that the student took such liberty with the youth group, surprised that a responsible student would do such a thing and disappointed that the student didn't know better. The student feels defensive that the supervisor is challenging her judgment and embarrassed and sad that she has let her supervisor down. Many of the most awkward or painful feelings arise from the way that the conflict challenges how each party would like to think of herself. As mentioned in the previous chapter on theological reflection, each of us would like to know ourselves as good, competent, and worthy of love. Conflict challenges our sense of identity. The student feels that her competence as a youth minister is being challenged because her decision to leave the youth group has come under scrutiny. The supervisor finds it difficult to confront the student because confrontation doesn't fit in with her idea of herself as a nice, friendly mentor. If, in a conflictual situation, the supervisor and student are able to become aware of how their interpretations, their feelings, and their senses of identity are playing a role in the tension, they will be able to bring the conversation to a new level of depth and honesty, making the chance of truly resolving the conflict much more possible.

5. *Practice curiosity.* Among the many virtues needed to be a person of reconciliation, curiosity ranks at the top, but is often the most underestimated. Curiosity is a genuine desire to understand what happened in a situation and why the other person acted and responded as he did.

Curiosity should also help me wonder why I acted and responded the way that I did. It asks real questions rather than rhetorical ones, and it doesn't pose any question to which it doesn't really want to hear the answer. Curiosity is most important in the beginning of a conversation about a conflict. It includes asking, "Can you tell me about your understanding of what took place?" "Can you say more about your intent?" "Can you talk to me more about why you chose that course of action?" But it is also very important at the end to ask, "Can you tell me what might persuade you to change your mind on this matter?" "What do you think the best course of action would be?" Curiosity asks these questions not as an avenue to insert one's own opinion, but to really learn about the other's point of view.

6. *Understand that intent and impact are two different things.* We usually know what we intend when we act, but we do not really have any control over how our actions are received by others—in essence, how our actions impact them. In reverse, we know how others' actions impact us, but we do not really ever know what their intent was. Intent and impact are two different things, but in conflict we often mistake them as one. If we are hurt by a situation, we often assume the other person intended to do so. If we really intended the best for another, we are shocked when they receive our goodwill less than gratefully. One of the most helpful things to do in the midst of a conversation about a conflict is to separate out intent from impact by making statements like, "I intended _____, but can you tell me how these actions impacted you?" or "I was really hurt by your words, but I doubt that is what you intended. Can you say more about your intentions?"

7. *Avoid the desire to blame.* Often, one of our unconscious hopes in conflict is that we will have the opportunity

to point out to the other person where he went wrong and he will readily accept the blame. Of course, this rarely happens, and more often than not, conversations that begin with this hope rapidly deteriorate. If we are genuinely convinced that conflict is an opportunity for learning, then the purpose of the conversation is not to assign blame, but to better understand what really happened so that we can make changes for the future. Blame seeks to place responsibility on one person in the tension, and it attributes to this person some sort of intentional moral shortfall. It places persons in a defensive position, and even if they were to accept that something was their "fault," it doesn't help them understand why the conflict happened nor ensure that it won't happen again.

It is much more useful to look at the situation from the perspective of an outside observer and analyze what role all of the parties and even external factors played in the situation's happening as it did. Not all of these factors were intentional. They were not all rooted in moral shortcomings. And they were not even all necessarily controllable. Each person in the conflict and, furthermore, the site itself contributed something to the conflict. This is not to say that they all share fault, simply that something they brought to the situation helped to shape it as it is. Referring back to the example of the unattended youth group, the student can acknowledge leaving the group without a chaperone and her unawareness that this would be a problem. Looking through the lens of contribution, the supervisor might become aware that he assumed the student would be aware of the dangers of unsupervised youth and didn't really orient the student to the parish's expectations. Looking at the situation from this perspective moves toward concrete steps that could be taken to make sure nothing similar happens again.

This is a much more effective resolution than simply knowing who is "at fault."

In the examples following this section, you will find an outline for working through a conflict that integrates these seven principles of healthy conflict. The first example offers questions that one could use to prepare for a conversation about a conflict. The second example offers a structure for the conversation itself. Perhaps you will never need to refer to these as a supervisor, but if you do, know that by entering into this level of respectful and honest conversation, you are offering your students one of the best preparations for healthy ministry they will ever have.

Preparation for a Difficult Conversation

Before raising a difficult topic with a student, it is often helpful to reflect on the situation for oneself first. The following questions can assist with preparing for the conversation:

- What is my version of the story?
- How might the other describe his or her version of the story?
- What is the "third story" (i.e., the way that a neutral outsider would summarize the story)?
- What were my intentions?
- What impact did the other's words and actions have on me?
- What might the other's intentions have been?
- What impact did my words and actions have on the other?
- What did I contribute to the problem?

- What did the other contribute to the problem?
- What else might have contributed to the problem?
- What feelings do I have about this situation?
- How does what happened threaten my concept of myself as a competent person who tries to do what is good and is worthy of love?

Outline for a Difficult Conversation

This model is based on *Difficult Conversations: How to Discuss What Matters Most* by Douglas Stone, Bruce Patton, and Sheila Heen.

Opening

1. Start from the "third story" (i.e. how a neutral outsider would summarize the conflict).

    I've been thinking about what happened last _____. There was a lot of tension when the meeting ended, and we haven't had a chance to talk since then . . .

    One of the requirements for the practicum that you are enrolled in is that you spend sixty-five hours on-site during the semester. When you submitted your time sheet, it struck me that you and I might have a different idea of what constitutes time spent on-site . . .

2. Share your purposes for the conversation (i.e., learning her story, expressing your views and feelings, problem-solving together).

    I'm wondering if we could talk about _____. I'd like to better understand what happened from your point of view and share with you how I felt about the event.

3. Invite the other to join you as a partner in sorting out the situation together.

I'm hoping you and I together could figure out some way that we could avoid repeating what took place again.

I'd like the two of us to think of ways that our supervisory relationship this semester could be most helpful to your growth as a minister, but in a time frame that would be manageable for me.

Middle

1. Listen with curiosity and openness to understand the other's perspective on the situation. Acknowledge any feelings that you hear underlying what he or she says.
   Can you tell me what you were thinking when _____?
   It sounds like you felt _____.
   What impact did my response have on you?
   Could you say more about why this is important to you?
2. Share your own point of view, your intentions, your feelings, and the impact that the other person's actions had on you.
   I felt both _____ and _____. I realize that these emotions may seem contradictory, but I want to get all of them out on the table.
   Though I hear you saying you received it as unjust criticism, I want you to know that my intention was _____.
   I recognize that each of us contributed to this situation, and I want to acknowledge that I could have spoken up earlier about the fact that this was bothering me . . .
3. Continue to "reframe" in order to keep the conversation on track. Reframe truth to perception, blame to contribution, and accusations to feelings.
   It sounds like you felt . . .
   You see my contribution to the problem as . . .
   I'm not looking to place blame. I'm hoping that we can better understand what each of us contributed to the situation being what it is.

Wrapping Up

1. Look toward options that meet each side's most important concerns and interests.
   I hear that _____ is really important to you, and I've expressed that _____ is really important to me. I'm wondering if we could think of a way that both of our needs could be met.
   Is there anything I could offer that would persuade you otherwise? If so, what would that be?
2. Talk about ways to keep communication lines open as you go forward.
   If something like this comes up again, what would be a good way for the two of us to handle it?
   When you are feeling this way again, could you bring it to me earlier so that perhaps we could discuss it sooner?

Ministerial Boundaries

The negotiation of healthy ministerial boundaries is an ongoing challenge for most ministers. Is it okay to go golfing with a parishioner on my day off? Should I say "yes" to another request, or do I need to draw the line and say "no"? Is it all right to bring my kids to work with me in a pinch? Can I spiritually direct a friend? Should I share with the mother of a youth group member what her teen revealed during a retreat? Establishing boundaries is especially challenging for field education students, many of whom are transitioning for the first time from a strictly voluntary ministerial role in a community to a more professional ministerial role and have not yet wrestled with the implications of this shift for their relationships.

All ministers—including ministry students—find themselves in **four basic types of relationships**. The first is **the professional pastoral relationship**—where one is on the "giving end" of care. The professional pastoral relationship is one of unequal power. The minister possesses knowledge, expertise, or access to resources (either physical or spiritual) that the other person in the relationship needs. In these relationships, the minister seeks to be of service to the other. It is largely a one-directional relationship. The minister has an obligation to listen carefully and to hold confidential anything that is shared, even when the other is not bound by the same degree of confidentiality. The minister bears primary responsibility for attending to boundaries that protect the other. The minister is aware of whatever feelings are going on inside of him but generally will not share them with the other unless it is for the other's benefit. He may also be able to relate easily from his own life with what the other is going through but, again, will not share his own life story unless it in some way will help the other. The focus of the relationship is service *to* the other.

A second type of relationship that ministers enter into is **colleagueship with professional peers**. The nature of the relationship is not primarily pastoral. It is one in which the minister works *with* others to meet a ministerial need. The relationship serves an end that is outside of itself; it is a two-directional relationship for the sake of a third. The relationship between the ministers is one of equal power. The ministers listen to each other, but the conversation is generally at the level of sharing ideas rather than sharing feelings. Confidentiality where necessary is to be expected. Ministerial staffs, for instance, share this peer relationship. Everyone on the staff may be a minister, but they are not ministers *to* each other; they are ministers *with* each other.

A third type of relationship that ministers enjoy is **friendship**. Strictly speaking, when in a friend relationship, the person is no longer functioning as a minister. In friendship, there is no power differential. Both partners in the relationship are free to share openly about their lives, feelings, and ideas as they choose. Confidentiality regarding anything personal is expected. It is a two-directional relationship in which the needs of both are mutually met. Family relationships, while certainly distinctive, share much in common with friendship relationships in that they are mutual and two-directional. The relationships within a family serve not just one person but all those involved.

The last type of relationship is a **reverse of the professional pastoral relationship** described earlier, where one is now on the "receiving end" of care. In this relationship, again, the person is no longer functioning as a minister, but rather in a relationship in which one can be ministered to. The onus of responsibility for listening, attending to boundaries, and confidentiality falls now on the other. The focus can be on oneself.

The first step in establishing healthy boundaries as a minister is identifying the type of relationship in which one is engaged. Often these categories can be a bit blurred for students in the beginning. It is difficult to see the difference, for example, between being friendly and being a friend. Or to distinguish between when one is to be in service *to* another versus *with* another. Or to note the difference between what one can say when one is a member of a congregation versus when one is the public face of the congregation. Some examples of boundary confusion in field education might include the following:

- Sharing too much of one's life story with a client, meeting a personal need to share rather than the client's need

- Expressing a strong opinion in a meeting of the community, unaware of the added weight that the opinion bears because of one's status as a minister
- Developing a close relationship to some members of the community in a way that excludes others in the community who should have equal access to the minister
- Casually expressing disagreement with a church teaching while serving as a representative of the institution
- Expecting ministry to meet one's own needs in the process of meeting those of others
- Repeatedly bringing personal issues into the workplace or work issues into the family setting
- Dating a member of the community one is serving
- Meeting for pastoral purposes in places generally reserved for family and friends; for example, one's home or a pub or a car

The problem in each of the above instances is not the behavior itself (e.g., sharing one's life story) but the relational forum in which it takes place (the professional pastoral relationship). There is a time for most things under the sun; the real challenge is discerning when and where that time is. However, not all relationships are clear cut, nor are they static over time. Sometimes colleagues need pastoral counsel. Employment relationships at times evolve into friendships. A minister's therapist moves into the parish. Dual relationships are not always avoidable in ministry, and we often end up in more than one type of relationship with the same person. Field education is often the first place that students become aware of the complex relationships into which professional ministry inevitably draws them. Supervisors provide a great service when they call attention to the student's boundaries and invite the student to reflect on these boundaries. Where do they draw the line in their various types of relationships, and what kind of line is it? Permeable? Sketchy? Rigid? Solid but flexible?

Supervisory relationships are not themselves exempt from boundary questions. The supervisory relationship is one type of professional pastoral relationship. In this case, the supervisor sits in the role of the minister. This means that the supervisor is the one primarily responsible for setting and maintaining appropriate boundaries in the relationship. While supervisors can certainly grow and learn a lot in the relationship, the relationship should not be regarded as mutual; its primary intention is service of the student's learning and growth. Sometimes at the end of a placement, students and supervisors choose to continue to be in a relationship as professional peers or friends, but at least during the placement itself, it is important that the relationship remain in the professional pastoral category. Remember that part of your responsibility is to write an evaluation of the student for the program. Friends should never be asked to evaluate friends; it violates both the integrity of the evaluation and the integrity of the friendship.

Finally, supervision should not be merged with the roles of spiritual director, pastoral care giver, or therapist. All of these could be considered professional pastoral roles and share the ethics of a professional pastoral relationship, but each of these roles serves a slightly different purpose. The spiritual director serves a person's relationship with God. The pastoral care giver provides support in times of deep need and questioning. The therapist helps persons integrate the whole of their lives, especially those pieces that need healing, and find ways of living more freely and fully. Certainly supervision has moments in which it assists with all of the above, but none of these can supersede the primary purpose of supervision, which is the student's growth as a minister to a community. In the end, your role is not to care for the student's needs, but to help the student care for others' needs. Whereas pastoral care, spiritual direction, and therapy all focus on the individual person, supervision ultimately focuses on the community. Where this distinction has the biggest impact is in the expectations regarding confidentiality. When students see a spiritual director, pastoral care giver, or therapist, they should be free to be entirely vulnerable and trust that what they share will never go beyond the walls of the meeting room. When students are in supervision, they should know that the confidentiality in this relationship is not absolute and that, if the supervisor has any concerns, these will need to be shared with the student's field education or program director. If one person serves, for example, as both a student's spiritual director and supervisor, the integrity of both roles can be easily violated.

Whatever guidelines are helpful for your student to observe when functioning as a professional minister, observe in your relationship with your students as well. In other words, while ministering as a supervisor, relate to the student within the professional pastoral forum and, as much as possible, avoid other kinds of relating. For instance, do not hang out as friends, get romantically involved, offer spiritual direction, or ask the student to baby-sit until the supervisory relationship comes to an end. Where it is impossible to avoid a dual relationship with the student, be very clear about when in a conversation you are "switching hats." Do not become so close to a student that you lose objectivity. Practice good self-care to make sure your own needs are being met. Modeling good boundaries is the best way of teaching good boundaries.

Referral

Sometimes in the course of supervision, one of two things becomes clear. The first is the realization that your student might benefit from additional opportunities to process an issue with a spiritual director or a counselor in order to further her flourishing as a minister. The second is that your student has significant issues that really *must* be processed with a counselor or it will have a negative impact on her ministry. In the first case, referral of the student is advisable. In the second case, it is mandatory.

Referral is the process of broadening a student's ministerial and personal formation by encouraging the student to draw on the assistance of other pastoral professional relationships beyond supervision. It honors the boundaries of the supervisory relationship, recognizing that there are limits to what a supervisor is trained to provide. It shouldn't be viewed as abdicating one's responsibility and care for the student, but sharing that care with others who are better able to handle various pieces of it.[4] Referring a student to another pastoral professional doesn't mean that supervision has failed. In fact, it is a sign that supervision is working well: the supervision has opened up new insights and avenues for learning and growth.

Supervisors engage in informal referral all the time. They pass on a book that they think a student might find helpful. They encourage a student to go find out more about a topic from a fellow staff member or parishioner. Referring a student to a counselor or spiritual director, however, can be a much more sensitive affair. If you sense simply that the student might really benefit by exploring an insight or issue with a counselor or spiritual director, it is good to introduce the idea as a gift that the student might want to give to himself at this point in time. Offer the suggestion as an opportunity for both personal growth and professional development. For example, if, in theological reflection, the student repeatedly makes connections to a parent who died years ago, you may begin to wonder whether there is still a lot of unresolved grief. It is okay to share what you are wondering with the student, as a "wondering" rather than a diagnosis, and let the student know about counseling resources you are aware of in the community that he might find helpful. In this situation, you are not concerned about the student's functioning as a minister but want to make him aware of possibilities and opportunities that perhaps he was not aware of before.

Should a serious issue surface, however, that makes you question a student's suitability for public ministry at this particular time, a more formal referral and follow-up that involve the student's field education or program director are in order. Situations in which the field education or program director should be contacted include the following:

- evidence of addictive behavior (abuse of gambling, alcohol, drugs, sex, etc.)
- suspicion of personal injury or eating disorder
- prolonged depression, increasing lack of emotion
- repeated episodes of overwhelming anxiety
- incapacitating guilt
- extreme difficulty in making routine decisions
- repeated or serious loss of self-control (outbursts of anger, weeping, etc.)
- phobias that affect how one interacts with others
- spiraling personal problems
- inability to adjust to change or to relax
- inability to develop healthy interpersonal relationships
- ongoing lack of concentration that impedes work
- extreme dependency or desire to please others
- expressed suicidal intentions

- any indication of pedophilic or ephebophilic inclinations
- any sign of severe mental disturbance (e.g., illusions of grandeur, paranoia, hallucinations, disorientation, memory loss)

When ministers suffer from any of the above conditions, it can have profound effects on the community that they serve. It is important that the student's ministry formation program be aware of these symptoms so that the program can fulfill its obligation to the larger community. Alerting the program director does not necessarily mean that the student will be removed from ministry or from the program. Indeed, many gifted ministers have suffered from depression or alcoholism or the like. But it can help program directors be much more proactive in helping the student find appropriate assistance and be much better prepared when helping the student discern his call.

In these situations, it is best to first contact the student's field education or program director and allow this person to take the lead in the referral process with the student. Ministry programs generally have an established procedure for working with students in need of further referral and sometimes have a list of counselors with whom they have an ongoing relationship. When in doubt about whether an issue is significant enough to merit additional help, it is always a good idea to call the director and seek further advice.

Time Management

One of the most challenging facets of the ministerial life is time management. Somewhere out there, there may be ministers twiddling their thumbs and wondering how to occupy themselves, but if there are, they are well hidden. Most ministers buzz from one appointment or event to the next—answering phone messages while driving, trying to decide whether it is more important to respond to e-mail, prepare a talk, visit someone who is in trouble, or squeeze in time for prayer. Many ministers acknowledge the desire for a healthy, well-rounded life, but few seem to have found the elusive perfect balance.

Management of time is one of the most critical predictors of success in contemporary ministry. New ministers need to learn how to prioritize among tasks, discern between what is urgent and what is important, and figure out how to live with the stress of many expectations. There is no one recipe for a balanced life; different ministers use different proportions of varied ingredients. But you can tell when something has gone awry. Like a bowling alley, while there is a wide acceptable aisle, there are gutters on either edge of that aisle. In the game of time management, those gutters are "burnout" and "rustout." Burnout is the combination of great amounts of work with unreasonable expectations of self that results in exhaustion, disappointment, and increasing cynicism. Rustout is a heightened focus on one's own needs and development over the legitimate demands of the ministry. The minister is so focused on self-care that other-care is consistently relegated to second place. Supervisors need to be alert to signs of either burnout or rustout in their students. Sometimes students will put way too much time into their field placement, to the detriment of their other work obligations, their studies, family, or community life. Sometimes they will have a hard time putting in their field education hours because they are having a hard time juggling the others. And sometimes their focus on making sure their lives stay in balance will be so predominant that you might wonder whether they really have the heart of a minister.

One good tool to help keep students accountable for their field education commitments, as well as to monitor potential for burnout or rustout, is a simple time chart. Where it would be helpful, ask students to track their time on-site and make general notes on how that time was spent. Have them bring their charts to your regular meetings with one another. In looking over the chart, you will be able to tell whether a student is working too many hours or too few and whether the student is allocating her time appropriately. Is she giving some things more time than they are probably worth? Is he getting caught up in the urgent versus the important?

Of course, the great challenge for supervisors is modeling good time management themselves. As with good boundaries, students will learn much more by what you do than by what you say about balancing time. Does the student see you block off on your schedule a day each week, that is not to be violated except for emergencies? Do they see you exercising not only firm boundaries on your time, but also flexible enough boundaries to accommodate the unexpected? Do they see you setting apart time to work on important processes like homily preparation or long-range planning or staff faith sharing, or are these things quickly put on the back burner when there is a time crunch? Is theological reflection time frequently canceled? Are communal prayer times often skipped? It is in the area of time management that students often surprisingly provide challenges to their supervisors instead of the other way around!

Cross-cultural Considerations

It will come as no surprise to anyone reading this chapter to hear that the Catholic Church in the United States is becoming more culturally diverse. Whereas 90 percent of U.S. Catholics who grew up before the Second Vatican Council and 85 percent of those who grew up alongside the Council are Anglo in ethnicity, only 50 percent of U.S.

Catholics born after the Council are non-Hispanic Anglos.[5] The ministerial face of the Catholic Church is changing more slowly, but still significantly. In the academic year 2005–2006, more than one-third of seminarians were non-Anglo, as were 25 percent of candidates for the diaconate and 21 percent of lay ministry students.

Ethnic Diversity in U.S. Ministry Formation Programs[6]

2005–2006	Seminarians	Deacon Candidates	Lay Ecclesial Ministry Candidates
Anglo	64%	75%	79%
Black	5%	3%	3%
Latino / Hispanic	15%	17%	12%
Asian	10%	4%	3%
Other	6%	1%	3%

Perhaps most significantly, a full quarter of the seminarians preparing for priesthood in U.S. seminaries are foreign born. About 16 percent of these seminarians intend to return to a diocese or religious community in another country, but 84 percent intend to serve in the United States. These seminarians represent 84 different countries, many with very different worldviews, traditions, and values from the dominant U.S. culture.[7]

At the same time, persons working in formation for ministerial students remain predominantly Anglo. Statistics from 2004 indicate that 92 percent of faculty serving in ministry schools is of Anglo heritage.[8] While no studies have been conducted specifically on the ethnic and cultural background of field education supervisors, it seems safe to suggest that the background of supervisors more closely mirrors that of the faculty population than that of the current student population. Chances are very likely that if you supervise multiple ministry students over time, you will be mentoring someone who does not share your ethnicity or, possibly, your country of origin.

Cross-cultural supervision brings with it many unique gifts, but also some unique challenges. The experience consistently highlights how much we take for granted in our day-to-day lives. So much of what we think is normal, right, and good we believe to be shared by all, or at least all who share our faith. In fact, much of what we consider to be common sense or appropriate behavior is shaped far more by cultural norms than religious ones. Even our definitions of what healthy ministry or good theological reflection look like are more culturally conditioned than we often like to admit.

Several decades ago, the Dutch social psychologist Geert Hofstede completed a landmark study of well over a hundred thousand people from more than seventy different countries to help develop a four-dimensional model for understanding cultural differences.[9] Later, in a revision of his work, he added a fifth.[10] These dimensions, described briefly below, can help us become more aware of how our own cultural perspective is but one of multiple different ways that humans around the globe might view things:

The Individualism/Collectivism Dimension

Cultures with a strong individualist orientation make sharp distinctions between the self and the society. Ties between individuals are loose, as everyone is expected to look after himself and his immediate family first. Independence, self-reliance, and personal financial stability are highly valued, while signs of dependency are regarded as unhealthy. Personal goals receive priority over communal ones. In cultures with a strong collectivist orientation, however, communal goals receive primary attention. In these societies, individuals are immediately integrated into very strong extended families from the time they are born. They will continue to depend upon these families throughout life and owe them unquestioning loyalty. Money and goods will be shared rather than saved for oneself. They are used to strengthen relationships, which are considered a stronger safety net than a private bank account. Simple differences in language constructs may bear witness to fundamental differences in individualist/collectivist cultures. In English, I would introduce myself saying, "My name is. . . ." In Spanish, however, I would say, "Me llama . . ." which would be more commonly translated, "I am called" or "they call me." The former reveals a focus on self, whereas the latter reveals a focus on the collective to which one belongs (i.e., the extended family or community).

The High/Low Power Distance Dimension

In cultures with a high sense of power distance, inequality within society is accepted as a fact of life. Persons with power are entitled to that privilege; those who do not have power cannot expect the situation to be any different. Authority is valued and respected and should not be questioned. In cultures with a low sense of power distance, inequality is viewed as problematic, and it is desirable to minimize differences as much as possible. Everyone is regarded as having the right to speak and to question authority. Low power distance societies believe that change within society is readily possible. Sometimes authority figures in low power distance societies may dress casually and act informally as a way of trying to not appear "uppity" or superior to others. Persons from high power distance societies, however, may find this effort confusing or even offensive, thinking, "Surely, this person owns better apparel. Do they not find us worthy enough to dress up for?" Persons who do not behave as their role in society expects are not necessarily seen as more approachable, but rather lacking professionalism and credibility.

The Masculinity/Femininity Dimension

Hofstede's study revealed that, globally, women share largely similar values, with an emphasis on modesty, caring, and cooperation. In more "feminine" cultures, women and men share these values, and gender roles are not emphasized. "Masculine" cultures, in contrast, make strong distinctions based on gender roles. Men are expected to be competitive, assertive, and ambitious, whereas women are expected to honor the more "feminine values" named above. Women in masculine cultures tend to be more assertive and competitive than women in feminine cultures, but not so much as the men in masculine cultures. Consequently, a gender-based value gap exists in masculine societies that doesn't exist in feminine societies.

The Uncertainty Avoidance/Acceptance Dimension

The uncertainty avoidance/acceptance index tries to measure a culture's comfort level with ambiguity and unstructured situations. Cultures marked by strong uncertainty avoidance find ambiguity undesirable and anxiety producing. These cultures develop strict, detailed rules and rituals to help create structured, predictable situations and decrease the possibility of unstructured situations ever arising. In philosophy and religion, they articulate belief in absolute Truth and the conviction that they possess it. Uncertainty acceptance cultures value spontaneity and change. They prefer to have as few rules as possible because creativity is a higher value than order. These cultures tolerate a variety of opinions and believe that persons with multiple points of view can still live in harmony. In philosophy and religion, they tend toward more relativist approaches.

The Long-Term/Short-Term Orientation Dimension

Cultures marked by a long-term orientation value long-term commitments. Hard work and perseverance are looked upon most favorably. Persons who are diligent and thrifty are praised. The amount of work that goes into a final product is often more important than the final product itself. In cultures marked by a short-term orientation, however, flexibility and the capacity to shift energies where needed are highly valued. Efficiency is highly praised. Genius is exalted over perseverance. Effort should be in proportion to the value of the project; it is not necessarily a good in itself.

Hofstede notes that each of these dimensions can be understood as a sliding scale. No culture is entirely individualist in its orientation, and no culture is entirely collectivist. But each culture can find its place somewhere along the continuum between the two poles. In Hofstede's work, the dominant culture of the United States is most defined by individualism. Its mark in this category—91—is higher than that of any other country in the world. The U.S. culture also tends toward the masculinity pole with a score of 62, whereas the world average is 50. On the power distance scale, the dominant culture of the United States leans toward the low side with a mark of 40; the global average is 55. On the uncertainty scale, the United States leans slightly toward the acceptance pole with a score of 46, in comparison to a global average of 64. In the area of term orientation, the United States demonstrates a clear preference for the short with a mark of 29, where the world average is 45.[11]

This information raises interesting questions for the discipline of ministerial field education: Are our judgments about students' behavior in and aptitude for ministry or theological reflection based on some sort of objective standard or a culturally conditioned one? Are our students understanding our actions and words as what we intend them? Are we interpreting our students' actions and words in the way they were intended? How do we honor each student's unique cultural heritage while at the same time honoring our own, not to mention the community's? The very process of theological reflection described in chapter 3 requires that the student have the capacity to stand outside of oneself and objectively reflect upon the "I" who is doing ministry. Is this process inherently biased toward an individualist perspective in which the "I" is looked upon as distinct from society? Similarly, are the signs that we discussed as indicators of a student needing additional psychological help biased toward independence and self-sufficiency over dependence on community? When I expect students to "speak up" in group theological reflection and take initiative to come see me about a problem, is that good adult education or simply Anglo adult education? What about when I expect a student to look me in the eye? Or set a firm deadline for when the learning contract is due or the time a supervisory appointment is to begin?

The more that we learn about cross-cultural communication, the more we realize that the possibilities for misunderstanding, insensitivity, and offense are endless, even when we have the very best of intentions—perhaps *especially* when we have the very best of intentions. It would be impossible here in a few short pages to create a fail-proof list of "dos" and "don'ts" for good cross-cultural supervision. It would be impossible even if we had hundreds of pages. This is an area about which there is so much to say but even more yet to learn, and we make progress humbly and slowly, usually by making many mistakes. Having said this, however, we can highlight three general principles that may be of use:

First, in all supervisory relationships, it is important to assume little. In cross-cultural supervisory relationships it is important to assume even less.

At the beginning of the placement, it is always good to ask the student to tell you about himself and what he feels it would be helpful for you to know about his life and background. In a cross-cultural relationship, this will be even more important. You might want to ask if the student recommends any particular books, articles, music, websites, art displays, or experiences in order for you to understand his culture better. Ask about preferences in the five dimensions of Hofstede's analysis. Be especially attentive when developing the learning contract to discuss the style of supervision that the student is expecting, what the "house rules" of the site are, and how the two of you will handle differences of opinion and conflict that emerge during the placement. The more explicitly these matters are discussed, the more assumptions will come to light and the less chance for misunderstanding.

Second, as the placement moves forward, continue to cultivate within oneself a perpetual curiosity, and encourage the student to model this attitude as well.

Interpretation and judgment are critical human faculties; we could not make it through the day without being able to exercise these functions. In cross-cultural supervision, though, we need to first practice pausing and wondering before interpreting and judging. Whenever something puzzles us, we need to check it out with the student in the form of a question rather than guessing we know the answer. As stated earlier, offenses and mistakes happen quite frequently in cross-cultural encounters, even among very well-intentioned people. It helps if, from the start, we just assume that these things will happen and that they are the fruit of genuinely different perspectives and unawareness, not ill will, maliciousness, carelessness, or ineptitude. To use an image from the Reagan era, it helps to develop "Teflon coating"—to not take things personally but instead respond, "Huh . . . I wonder . . ." And really do wonder.

Lastly, be conscious about initiating the student into the culture of the community that you are serving together.

Ministry, by its nature, is always other-centered. While we inevitably receive much from being in ministry, it is not in the end about meeting our own needs but meeting others' needs. While it is important in this professional ministerial relationship for the supervisor to respect and honor the student's culture, it is just as important—if not even more important—for the student and supervisor together to respect and honor the culture of the community they serve. How is time observed in this community? How much personal space do people need to be comfortable? What kinds of boundaries do people expect? How are meetings run? How are decisions made? Are you expected to take off your shoes when you enter a home? Should you bring a gift if invited to dinner? All cultures stand in need of conversion and transformation. But, as ministers, when we speak prophetically and try to shift a custom of the community, we do it not so that it accommodates the minister better, but so it accommodates the Gospel better. Becoming familiar with a community's history and interviewing community members as part of the field placement can really help deepen a student's knowledge of and appreciation for the local culture.

One of the greatest gifts of cross-cultural supervision is the richness of theological reflection that can take place. Again, all students bring a different perspective to reflection that is enlightening to hear, but the perspective from someone of another ethnicity or culture can be especially enriching. Be certain to take full advantage of this opportunity by making multicultural analysis a component of every reflection that the two of you undertake. How would the student's culture understand the dynamics of the situation? How would the supervisor's culture make sense of what is going on? How would the community likely perceive the event? An extraordinary amount can be learned in these conversations by the supervisor as well as by the student.

Summary

The topics addressed in this chapter are some of the most challenging ones that emerge in the work of ministerial field education. They are also some of the most exciting. As noted at the opening of the chapter, when these issues surface in a placement, you know that field education is really doing what it is intended to do: facilitate insight, awareness, learning, and growth. It is stretching the student in new directions. It is also, inevitably, stretching the supervisor, which brings us to the final chapter of this book.

Questions for Reflection and Discussion

1. In this chapter, five common issues that surface in field education were introduced: *conflict, ministerial boundaries, referral, time management,* and *cross-cultural communication.* With which of these issues are you already well familiar from your own experience of ministry? Which is a new

consideration for you? Are there other common issues that you would like to see addressed?

2. What wisdom from your own experience would you like to add to the author's comments on any of the five issues? Is there any topic that you view differently?

3. Which of the following descriptors best matches how you feel about supervision after reading this chapter?

- increasingly enthused
- nervous
- concerned
- more aware
- overwhelmed
- empowered
- other _____

Why did you choose this descriptor?

4. What questions do you have after reading this chapter? What kinds of resources are available to you to help with these questions?

CHAPTER 4 NOTES

1. The following principles are offered and treated in greater detail in Loughlan Sofield and Carroll Juliano, *Collaboration: Uniting Our Gifts in Ministry* (Notre Dame, IN: Ave Maria Press, 2000), 124–127.

2. C.S. Lewis, *A Grief Observed* (New York: Harper, 1961), 34.

3. A number of books make similar points about healthy conflict and confrontation, but I want to acknowledge that I am particularly indebted here to the work of the Harvard Negotiation Project—specifically, Douglas Stone, Bruce Patton, and Sheila Heen, *Difficult Conversations: How to Discuss What Matters Most* (New York: Penguin Books, 1999).

4. Howard Clinebell, *Basic Types of Pastoral Care and Counseling* (Nashville: Abingdon Press, 1984), 311.

5. Mary Gautier, "Parishes Past, Present, and Future: Demographic Realities" in *Multiple Parish Pastoring in the Catholic Church in the United States: Symposium Report* (Emerging Models of Pastoral Leadership Project, February 2006), 20–21; available at www.emergingmodels.org.

6. Center for Applied Research in the Apostolate (CARA), *Catholic Ministry Formation Enrollments: Statistical Overview for 2005–2006* (Washington, DC: Georgetown University, 2006); available at http://cara.georgetown.edu.

7. Ibid, 11.

8. Katarina Schuth, "Diversity and the Formation for Ministry: Understanding the Challenge" in *Educating Leaders for Ministry*, ed. Victor Klimoski et al. (Collegeville, MN: Michael Glazier Books, 2005), 13.

9. Geert Hofstede, *Culture's Consequences: International Differences in Work-Related Values* (Beverly Hills, CA: Sage Publications, 1980).

10. Geert Hofstede and M. Bond, "Confucius and Economic Growth: New Trends in Culture's Consequences," *Organizational Development* 16, no. 4, (1988), 4–21. An overview of all five dimensions with an analysis of how more than fifty different countries score using these indexes can be found at www.geert-hofstede.com.

11. ITIM International, "Geert Hofstede Cultural Dimensions" (accessed 28 December 2006); available at www.geert-hofstede.com.

The Spirituality of the Supervisor

The focus of this book has been the professional ministerial relationship that exists between the supervisor and field education student. As reiterated several times, this is a relationship that is—as with all ministerial relationships—other centered. Supervision is a ministry to the student and to the community. We are not able to expect that our own personal needs or even our institution's work needs will always be met in taking on a field education student. Ministry is a gift given without strings attached. At the same time, we cannot deny that, in the mysterious graciousness of God, whenever we minister, we do receive in return. Not always what we expected, but a gift nonetheless—often a greater gift than what we were able ourselves to offer. In theological language, we might say that ministry is praxis: it is self-transforming activity.

Much is written about spirituality. Some of the literature makes it sound as if the life of the spirit were somehow quite separate from daily life, with its traffic and meetings and clogged plumbing. It focuses on that part of the day, week, or year that we can dedicate to silence, to being "away from it all," to stepping out of the chaos and morass of our routine existence. And yet, while time for silence and retreat is *very* valuable and necessary, at the heart of the Catholic sacramental tradition lies the conviction that God loves the world. God chooses to make Godself known to us through created matter. God is known in the matter of bread and wine, water and oil, but also the matter of our lives, our families, our work, and our congregations. While there are many conceivable ways of defining spirituality, one possibility is simply to say that spirituality is the particular way in which God works out our salvation in this world—in essence, the particular way in which God brings us into the fullness of life and light for which we are intended. So, if we speak of a Christian spirituality, we mean that Jesus Christ plays an integral role in our salvation. If we speak of a marital spirituality, we mean that it is through the experience of being married that God intends to make us into the people that we are meant to be. If we speak of a ministerial spirituality, we pause to reflect on how, through the practice of ministry, God is transforming the minister. And if we speak then of the spirituality of the supervisor, the key question we will want to ask is, "How is the ministry of supervision somehow part of the way that God is transforming me into the person God dreams me to be?"

In the Judeo-Christian tradition, to receive a vocation or a call from God is an invitation to movement. In Genesis, the first words that God speaks to Abraham are "Come out" (Gn 12:1). In John, the Good Shepherd "calls his own by name and leads them out" (Jn 10:3). Calls impel us "out" of ourselves to something more, something beyond. As Margaret, a character in Gail Godwin's novel *Evensong*, points out, "Something is your vocation if it keeps making more of you."

While supervision is likely not going to be your primary vocation in life, it is a call from the Church, and from God.

It can be a powerfully transformative experience. And it may very well be that you will discover your own spiritual journey is deeply intertwined with your willingness to serve in this ministry. God plans to do things through this experience, not just for the student, but for you, too.

The experience of each supervisor is unique and particular, and yet, when experienced supervisors talk about "the more" that supervision has made of them, they often mention eight key virtues or dispositions that the practice of the ministry seems to inherently cultivate if we allow it:[1]

Supervision calls us to wholeness. When we are charged with challenging and forming others to be healthy and whole ministers, we will be immediately confronted with all those ways in which *we* are not as healthy and whole as we should be. When we ask tough questions to others, we begin also to ask tough questions of ourselves. For example, "How can I talk with a student about developing better balance in her life when I work seventy hours a week?" "How can I suggest a student go talk with a counselor about possible depression when I've always avoided counselors myself?" "How can I give lectures on good conflict management when I absolutely refuse to deal constructively with another coworker?" As we hold up the mirror for students, students often unwittingly hold the mirror up to us. We realize where greater personal integrity is needed between what we advocate and what we actually do. Supervision makes us attentive to aspects of our own life that we might otherwise overlook.

Parents often give up certain vices, such as smoking or cursing or watching excessively violent television shows, once their children begin to imitate those behaviors. Behaviors that seem somewhat innocuous to adults or are only perceived to affect oneself suddenly appear glaringly inappropriate when someone new, someone they care about, begins to try them on for size. Similarly, in supervision, for the sake of the next generation, one feels a renewed urgency to "clean up" bad ministerial habits. Things that we might not do for ourselves, we do for those who are looking to us as models.

Supervision calls us to humility. Supervision can make us aware of how much we have learned and grown over time in ministry. Tasks that a new student might find difficult, we suddenly realize, have become very easy for us. We become aware of how many gifts we have for ministry and how much knowledge we've acquired. But, just as often, the experience of supervising makes us aware of our own shortcomings and limitations. Many times, we will sit in front of students who are good, holy, and talented people and think, "Who I am to be giving them advice? I don't know the answer any more than they do" or "Who am I to be making judgments about whether this person should go on in ministry? I don't know enough about this stuff. I am not God!" Many supervisors find that the process of evaluation and offering constructive feedback is especially humbling: "How can I name a splinter in the student's eye when I may have a plank in my own?"

As noted in chapter 3, a student's sense of identity as a minister is often marked by an "all-or-nothing" mentality. He thinks either he is good or he is bad. Either he is competent or he is incompetent. In truth, many of us in the field of supervision consider ourselves through the same black and white lens. Either I must be a perfect supervisor or I have nothing to offer. Either I must have excellent judgment or I shouldn't judge at all. The truth is that none of us is as wonderful a mentor as we would like to be, and none of us has perfectly clear judgment and full knowledge of a student's abilities and character. We often become more aware of our own imperfections than of theirs. And then we gradually learn to live with ourselves honestly and openly, acknowledging what "mixed bags" we are. The poet May Sarton writes:

> Now I become myself.
> It's taken time, many years and places.
> I have been dissolved and shaken,
> worn other people's faces. . . .
> As slowly as the ripening fruit,
> fertile, detached, and always spent,
> falls but does not exhaust the root.[2]

Supervision, if we allow it, helps us become ourselves and become okay with those selves.

Supervision calls us to courage. A commonly repeated joke tells of a mother coming in to wake up her son for school. The son pulls the sheets over his head and whines, "I don't want to go. I don't like school. All the kids make fun of me and are mean to me." "You will go to school," the mother retorts. "The sun is up, the bus is coming, and you have to go: you are the principal." This is how it is sometimes, isn't it? We wake up to find ourselves leaders and mentors of others without quite knowing how it happened. It can be rather overwhelming. The work asks us to tackle issues that we don't quite know how to handle—issues that take us far beyond our comfort zones. Many times a supervisor will suddenly realize, "I'm going to have to grow up to the job."

At this point, the virtue of humility in the supervisor must find its complement in the virtue of courage or fortitude. No, we don't know everything we wish we knew. No, we are not perfect. No, we don't feel worthy to make recommendations that could affect others' lives. But, with due humility, we also have to act. We have to ask difficult questions. We have to make decisions. We have to offer challenging feedback. Sometimes we even have to write negative evaluations and let the student know face to face. We struggle to cultivate a "response-ability" to match our responsibility.

Often, as a field education director, I find myself in situations with students and supervisors that I would very much prefer to avoid. I know that I do not have the wisdom or experience that I should have to be dealing with the issues present, but nevertheless, there they are, and there I am. I do know enough from experience to know that no matter how badly I might botch things up through direct confrontation, it will be better than how badly I will botch things up by not directly confronting. This is often not much of a consolation. At these times, I must rely not on my own inner resources, but on the grace of the role itself. I recall that someone has asked me to serve in this capacity and appointed me to carry out the task. There may be someone better out there, but that person is not here right now, and the work needs to be done now. I have to trust that the gap between what the role requires and me will be filled by the Holy Spirit.

In his Second Letter to Timothy, there is a wonderful line in which Paul encourages Timothy to "stir into flame" the gift of God that Paul knows is within his disciple, reminding him that "the Spirit God has given us is no cowardly spirit, but rather one that makes us strong, loving, and wise" (2 Tm 1:6–7). That same Spirit is the one that bolsters field education supervisors all the time, making the work possible and effective. Supervisors come to know that the Spirit really is with them and within them, just waiting to be "stirred into flame."

Supervision calls us to trust. One of the key qualities that supervision cultivates is trust. At the beginning of a supervisory relationship, it can sometimes be hard to send the student off on her own, and we find ourselves wondering: "Wouldn't it be good for her to observe a little longer?" "What if he does something that offends the congregation?"

"What if she fails and I have to pick up the pieces?" It can be hard to turn over portions of our ministry to others and allow them to do it differently, to accept the possibility that things might go awry. As the placement proceeds, it can also be difficult to trust the process of field education itself: "Yes, theological reflection is good and all, but can't I just tell him the answer without having to go through a whole reflection?" "Can't I just fix the situation for her?" "Do I really have to wait for him to find his own answers and let him try something I am sure will flop?" But perhaps the greatest trust is called for at the end of the placement. Often supervisors feel that they have not done quite enough. "Does the student really know all that she needs to know to move into this field?" "Is he ready for ordination?" "Is she ready to be hired?" "Have I said all that I should have said?" "Is the future of the Church safe in his hands?"

One of the most challenging parts about being a supervisor is that supervisors don't often have a lot to show for their efforts at the end of their work. Unlike for an architect or a fundraiser, there is no physical building or financial report that bears witness to the supervisor's labor. The supervisor's efforts are directed toward a person of free will, who can accept what is offered or reject it or, often, can hear only part of what is being said. Sometimes the impact of a supervisor's message doesn't hit until years later. Words that didn't make sense at the time suddenly have meaning, but the supervisor is long gone. There is a certain poverty in serving in this ministry, and ultimately the final act of trust that the supervisor must make is that supervision really does make a difference. Author Laurie Beth Jones summarizes this aspect of the supervisor's spiritual journey well when she notes:

> Jesus did not say, "I've left construction of the temple in capable hands, and it should be finished by May." Nor did he say, "I've doubled the

number of your recruits here, and you will note the offerings are up in three locations." Instead his summary read: "Dear Chairman of the Board, as proof of my good work here, I present to you Peter, James, John, Mary, Mary Magdalene, and Martha . . . completed in love."[3]

Supervision calls us to curiosity and patience. When identifying virtues culled in supervision, almost every supervisor names patience. In supervision, there is a long waiting as the student slowly readies to reveal himself. This is a process that cannot be forced or rushed. Educator Parker Palmer testifies:

> Like a wild animal, the soul is tough, resilient, resourceful, savvy, and self-sufficient. . . . Yet, despite its toughness, the soul is also shy. . . . If we want to see a wild animal, we know that the last thing we should do is go crashing through the woods yelling for it to come out.[4]

If this is true of the search to encounter our own cores, imagine how much more so it is true when we attempt to touch the core of another. Trust in the supervisory relationship is built over time. Students do not generally jump into supervision eager to receive critique of their ministry and ask hard questions about their lives. Only gradually do they become aware of why these practices are necessary and what amazing fruits these practices can bear. Sometimes it is important to push a student, but just as many times, it is important to wait.

Patience is also required when a student is learning new skills and new behaviors. Experienced supervisors note that they have forgotten how much they'd learned over time until they see someone else take her first steps in the ministry. Occasionally new supervisors are shocked when their student doesn't seem to be aware of information they regard as common sense: "Well, of course, you wouldn't talk about a patient openly at the nurses' station." "Well, of course, you don't fill the wine carafe to the top; otherwise the communion ministers will be left to consume too much at the end." "Well, of course, there needs to be coffee present at the council meeting; without caffeine there will be a rebellion." Supervising over a long period of time, however, cultivates an added awareness of small stumbling blocks and a tolerance of mistakes.

The partner of patience is curiosity. Curiosity is a virtue that has been mentioned several times in this book and is one of the defining characteristics of excellent supervisors. At some point in time, many supervisors experience a shift from frustration and irritation with a student to genuine wonder. "Why did you *do* that?!" shifts to "*Why* did you do that?" "What were you *thinking*?!" becomes "What were *you* thinking?" Rhetorical questions are rephrased to become real queries. The greatest learning in field education happens when supervisors and students become truly curious, when they are able to stand back a bit from situations and say with the interest of a scientist or an artist, "Wow. What is going on here?"

Supervision calls us to reflection as a way of life. The practice of theologically reflecting on a regular basis has a profound impact on the lives of supervisors, sometimes even more than it does on students' lives! Experienced ministers who supervise over a number of years find that they enter into an ongoing reflective mode of being. Whereas once theological reflection was a time set apart to look at incidents in the student's experience, gradually theological reflection becomes a way of life—a permanent curiosity and wonder that constantly makes connections between personal experience, faith, and culture. Here is a typical observation:

I have become more in tune with theological reflection in my own life. It helps me make connections in my daily life and activities. I have become more open to the grace of the Holy Spirit being operative in me and others.

To use again the analogy of the night sky, when longtime supervisors look around them, they no longer see events like isolated stars on a dark backdrop. Rather, they see constellations—relationships among the stars that others might miss. They see patterns and bigger pictures in which all things are connected. When theological reflection truly becomes a *habitus,* it wires the brain to enable a new way of seeing.

Supervision calls us to embrace "death." To say that field education supervision invites us to embrace death can sound a bit melodramatic. Opportunities for physical martyrdom in the line of duty are very rare. And yet, as writer Vigen Guroian notes, "Our lives are filled with countless little intimations of death"[5]—in the waxing and waning of relationships, in the things that we must give up, the hopes we must let go. In ministerial leadership, one longtime supervisor confirms, "You die a thousand deaths for the good of the whole."

Among these deaths that supervisors are called to are some that we have already discussed. For example, supervisors experience a death of the ego when they come to a new awareness of their own shortcomings and limitations. And, they are called to "die to control" with the realization that the student and the field education process have a life of their own that supervisors can participate in, but never completely manage.

Perhaps the most subtle of these deaths is the death of productivity. Supervisors rarely have a lot of extra time in their schedules. If not supervising, there are always a hundred other things they could be doing. This means that supervisors generally must let go of something else that they wanted to do in order to fit in supervising a field education student. Maybe it is a book they wanted to read, a committee they would liked to have been part of, or a project they wanted to take on. Sometimes students need more attention and energy than anticipated. Sometimes their timing is not particularly good. They need to talk when the supervisor has a big deadline. Much of the ministry of supervision is in acceptance of the interruptions.

Each of these deaths—and innumerable others—could be skirted and ignored or greeted and welcomed. In every Christian vocation, there is an aspect of the Paschal Mystery. It is precisely through embracing this mystery and walking through it that our spiritual journeys actually become salvific. In a talk about staying alive and thriving as a leader of a ministerial institution, seminary president Charles Bouchard commented:

> Staying alive does not, ironically, mean avoiding death. It means facing death and risk, embracing them gracefully and in faith, and trusting that they will shape us into good servants who will lead our institutions [and, we could add, students] to all they can be.[6]

Supervision calls us to hope. Death never has the last word, however. Even supervisors who have faced great challenges, when asked to describe their students, inevitably use language like "fresh and energetic," "enthusiastic," and "full of zeal." One supervisor writes, "Working with students can refresh my spirit on days when I'm feeling jaded or cynical or have difficulty seeing the hand of God through the political aspects of Church work." Another acknowledges, "As I encounter the sincerity they bring with their desire to serve, I am touched by their holiness, goodness, and truth—albeit often different from my own. This helps me become more than what I was prior to this encounter." In the end, the most common comment of supervisors is something along the lines of, "The students give me hope." Hope that the message of Jesus Christ will go on. Hope that Christ's care will be extended in new ways. Hope that there truly are others who will carry on the ministry. Hope that others find their joy in the same thing that has made our lives so rich and meaningful. Some of the best, brightest, and most generous people in the world are hearing a call to service. Field education puts us in contact with them. There is plenty of reason for hope.

Field education, as a call from God and the Church, has the potential to "make more" out of us. It makes us more whole, more humble, and more courageous. It makes us more trusting, curious, and patient. It makes us more reflective. It marks on us the pattern of Christ, moving through death to hope in new life. The gift of the ministry is that it makes of us all of these things, not only when we are sitting in the role of the supervisor, but also in our daily lives. What we learn and practice in supervision begins to permeate our relationships with our peers, our families, and our communities. "Supervision has definitely led me to be a better person," writes one supervisor. "I am always grateful."

There are many scriptural images that supervisors use to capture the kind of relationship with God and others that supervision has called them into. These images illumine aspects of themes discussed in this chapter and range from the familiar, like Jesus and the Samaritan woman at the well, to the more obscure, like Tobias and the angel Raphael. They capture the dynamic of honesty and confrontation that exists in supervision, like Nathan before David, as well as the joy of sharing, like the story of the Visitation. Scripture is a gold mine full of rich models of mentoring. An exercise based on some of these scriptural images appears in appendix D as a way of reflecting further on the themes explored in this chapter and offering companions on the supervisory journey. When we struggle with embracing death, stirring the fire of courage, or finding hope, these are stories that we can return to again and again to light the path. Their characters are fellows in the company of saints who will draw aside and walk with us.

Perhaps the most challenging image depicting the spirituality of the supervisor is found in the story of the Prodigal Son from Luke 15:11–32. In his book *The Return of the Prodigal Son*, Henri Nouwen offers an extended meditation on Rembrandt's painting of that parable. The painting portrays the father's welcome of his wayward son while the elder, faithful son and three onlookers obscured in darkness stand by. Nouwen describes his long fascination with the picture and the relationship that he developed with each of its characters, seeing how each represented himself at various times in his life. He notes that initially he saw himself in the figure of the younger son, the one who squanders the family wealth and needs to seek forgiveness. With time, he came to know himself as the elder son—faithful and stable, but also resentful and jealous. The hardest character to identify with was the one at the center of the picture. He records the challenge of a friend who pointed out to him, "Whether you are the younger son or the elder son, you have to realize that you are called to become the father."[7]

Nouwen relays the shock and resistance he felt to first hearing these words and how long it took for him to grow comfortable with this new identity. "The year and a half since [my friend's] challenge has been a time to begin claiming my spiritual fatherhood," he writes. "It has been a slow and arduous struggle, and sometimes I still feel the desire to remain the son and never to grow old."[8] Later he writes:

Though I am both the younger son and the elder son, I am not to remain them, but to become the Father. No father or mother ever became father or mother without having been son or daughter, but every son and daughter has to consciously choose to step beyond [his or her] childhood and become father and mother for others. It is a hard and lonely step to take . . . but a step that is essential for the fulfillment of the spiritual journey.[9]

There are many ways in which engaging the metaphor of fatherhood in a book about supervision could go awry. In chapter 4, we discussed in detail why supervision should be construed as a professional and not a familial relationship; our students are not best viewed as prodigals, and the image will strike some as gender exclusive. Furthermore, in our culture, the language of "fatherhood" often immediately evokes images of *Father Knows Best*. That is not what we are talking about here.

The image of fatherhood that Nouwen is evoking is quite different. He is using the metaphor to touch on something very close to the heart of the supervisor's vocation: the call to generativity, the call to take up one's proper authority and become the leader.

For much of our lives, we speak of the Church in third person. "The Church teaches . . ." "The Church should be . . ." "The Church says . . ." And then there comes a moment when we realize that we actually *are* the Church, and if the Church should be doing anything, it should be us doing it. Nouwen notes that perhaps the most radical words Jesus spoke were, "Be compassionate as your Father is compassionate."[10] We are invited not just to turn to God *for* compassion, but also to *become* that compassion of God for others. In exercising the ministry of supervision, we will need to become comfortable, just as our students will, with modeling something of

God for others. "Christ has no body now but yours," echoes Teresa of Avila in her famous prayer.

"Becoming the father" does not mean exercising power that is in any way oppressive, abusive, or self-serving. That is not the kind of power that God has ever exercised. It does mean being willing to take on the power to reconcile, to love, to confront, to make decisions that serve the common good, to heal, to hope, to lay down one's life.

Summary

This book has been about the invitation to serve as a supervisor. In the end, that invitation is the invitation to "become the father"—to become the kind of minister the world needs in the process of mentoring the ministers that the world needs. If you believe in the future of the Church and its ministry, the work that you are about to undertake is absolutely essential. It is essential for the student. It is essential for the People of God. It may even be essential for you. Be ready for a spiritual adventure.

Questions for Reflection and Discussion

1. Do you consider the invitation to supervise a ministry student as part of your overall vocational journey?
2. How do you see God transforming you through your current ministerial role? In what ways do you suspect God might be inviting you to change and grow in taking on the role of a supervisor?
3. What most excited you when reading this chapter? What did you find frightening or uncomfortable?
4. What metaphor or image from scripture or tradition best captures the spiritual dynamic of supervision for you?

CHAPTER 5 NOTES

1. In preparing for this chapter, I interviewed several persons who have been involved in the Aquinas Institute field education program. I want to acknowledge with gratitude the following: Mary Joan Meyer, F.S.M.; Greg Rohde, Jackie Toben, S.S.N.D.; Steve Gira, C.R.; Julie Allen Berger; Celeste Mueller; Diane Kennedy, O.P.; Charles Bouchard, O.P.; Russell Peterson; and Bob Sweeney.

2. May Sarton, "Now I Become Myself," in *Collected Poems, 1930–1973* (New York: Norton, 1974), 156.

3. Laurie Beth Jones, *Jesus, CEO: Using Ancient Wisdom for Visionary Leadership* (New York: Hyperion, 1995), 286.

4. Parker Palmer, *A Hidden Wholeness: The Journey Toward an Undivided Life* (San Francisco: Jossey-Bass, 2004), 58.

5. Vigen Guroian, *Life's Living Toward Dying: A Theological and Medical-Ethical Study* (Grand Rapids, MI: Wm. B. Eerdmans Publishing, 1996), 22.

6. Charles Bouchard, O.P., "Death and the President," an address to the ATS-sponsored New Presidents' Seminar in New Orleans, January 2005.

7. Henri Nouwen, *The Return of the Prodigal Son* (New York: Doubleday, 1992), 22.

8. Ibid.

9. Ibid., 122.

10. Ibid., 123.

Sample Student Case Studies

In field education, students are asked to bring slices of their ministry experience to supervision for theological reflection. Below are sample student cases, representative of the kinds of issues that students might bring. Consider each case individually. How would you facilitate theological reflection on this case? What kinds of questions would you ask? What pitfalls would you want to avoid in your facilitation? What insights would you bring to the conversation?

Where possible, it may be helpful to role-play the case with another person playing the part of the student. Ask this person to give you feedback on your facilitation of the case afterward.

CASE #1

Student: Mary Clare

Brief Biography: Mary Clare is an Anglo, age twenty-nine, and a lifelong Catholic. She is interested in youth ministry and is currently interning with St. Bridget's Catholic Youth Council (CYC).

Site Description: St. Bridget's is a white, middle-class parish of about eight hundred families located on the outskirts of a major midwestern city. It has a vibrant grade school of about four hundred fifty students, K–8. From there, its graduates go on to any variety of local Catholic and public high schools. For years now, St. Bridget's has struggled to keep its teens active in the Church during high school. It has long had an active CYC group run by volunteer parents, with the perennial new young associate pastor serving as its spiritual adviser. For the first time, the parish no longer has a full-time young associate pastor. The last one was removed three years ago because of a sexual abuse scandal. It now has an older, part-time associate pastor who also has a part-time diocesan position. So, the CYC has been functioning with very little input from the parish clergy. The parish has no youth minister, director of religious education, or any salaried lay minister on staff at all.

Narrative for Reflection: Every winter, the CYC holds a fundraising show called the "Bridget Brigade." In years past, it has been a sort of talent show with short skits and musical numbers. A few years ago, when the CYC's membership was lagging and fewer parents were available and willing to lead the group, the father of one of the teens stepped forward and agreed to coordinate and direct the annual winter show. "Mr. X" is a professional musician who has his own rock band that performs in local bars around the city. He has continued to direct the show for the past three years, even after his own daughter graduated from high school. Under his direction, the CYC Bridget Brigade now has more teens participating in it than before. However, the nature of the Bridget Brigade has changed more into a sort of elaborate karaoke show in which the performing teens dress up in model-like clothing and sing solos in a microphone to a minus-one recording with other performers doing "air band" in the background. The songs are contemporary pop songs of their generation. The father has been able to add some dazzling special effects with lights and smoke, which are rented for the event.

When I came to the parish at the beginning of the spring semester, it was only one week before the show would be performed. I was with the teens, getting to know them during one of their final dress rehearsals, so I got to see what the show was going to be about. This winter, the show was called "A Tribute to Our Military Forces." The performers read passages on patriotism and the righteousness of war. All of the musical selections had some kind of connection to the post-9/11 United States or the military, except for one pacifist song from the 1960s in which all of the performers wore tie-dye and were playing drums, swaying, and pretending to smoke marijuana. Music included a song in which a woman sings about sleeping with a man other than her husband while he is overseas and Toby Keith's "Courtesy of the Red, White, and Blue," which includes lyrics about "kicking" other countries "in the ass."

When I saw the dress rehearsal, I felt very uncomfortable, not sure whether some of these things were appropriate for a church-sponsored youth show. I felt like maybe I should step up and say something, but it was only my first week in the parish.

CASE #2

Student: Carl

Brief Biography: Carl is a seminarian in his pastoral year—a year of full-time ministry, halfway through his seminary studies. Among other responsibilities, he's been asked to coordinate parish liturgies. He is Anglo, age thirty-three.

Site Description: Our Lady of Guadalupe Parish is a large, diverse West Coast parish with well-educated parishioners, many of whom work for the local university.

Narrative for Reflection: It is currently Year B in the liturgical cycle. Yesterday, on Friday afternoon, Inez, one of the new parish lectors, called me. She was preparing to read the second reading on the coming Sunday: Ephesians 5:21–32. "Carl," she said, "I won't read this reading unless I can skip the verses on 'wives be submissive to your husbands.' In my lifetime I have seen too much violence and abuse done to women, much of it by those who have regarded this verse as the Word of God. And I won't read on Sunday unless I can omit it." I agreed to run it by our pastor, who will be celebrating Sunday's 11 a.m. Mass. He responded, "Sunday's gospel says that there are 'hard words' in scripture. Many people, the Bible says, left Jesus because they thought his words were too hard. That's life. I'm not about to change the words of the scripture. She doesn't have to read them, but she also won't be lectoring for us any more."

I think that Inez is expecting me to call her back before tomorrow, but I am entirely unsure what to do or to say to her. I can see her point, and I can see the pastor's point, too. I feel totally trapped.

CASE #3

Student: Ted

Brief Biography: Ted is an African American, age sixty, who is in deacon formation for his diocese. He has taught senior theology at St. Scholastica's High School for five years since retiring from business. He is using his full-time job as his field education site.

Site Description: St. Scholastica's is a large suburban high school on the East Coast serving a lower-middle-class population.

Narrative for Reflection: For the last couple years, I've been the faculty adviser of the National Honor Society (NHS) for the school and chair the decision process by which new members are chosen for induction into the NHS. To belong to the NHS at St. Scholastica's is to belong to quite an elite group with very high standards. NHS members are expected to have a grade point average of 3.75 or above, possess high moral character, and demonstrate leadership ability. Generally, out of a class of two hundred, the committee is asked to pick only ten students for induction each year. Because the standards are so high, local colleges often fight over NHS students graduating from St. Scholastica's. These students have a very good chance of getting significant scholarships and financial aid after graduation.

My brother and his wife live in the vicinity of the school. They have five kids and have struggled to send them to the best Catholic schools possible. Neither has a college degree but has hoped that by giving their children a great education, the children will be able to get the kind of financial aid and scholarships they need to go on to good colleges.

My brother and his wife have one daughter, Cora, who is currently a sophomore at St. Scholastica. Cora is a straight-A student who has been active in student council and in the soccer program. Cora is popular with the teachers, who have noted strong leadership skills in her. I was not at all surprised when Cora was nominated by faculty members for induction into the NHS. The problem is that I know from

Cora's parents that they've been having lots of problems with Cora lately. They recently found out that on a night they thought Cora was spending the night over at a friend's house, she had actually spent the night at her boyfriend's house when the boyfriend's parents were away on a trip. Also, when I was over at my brother's house a few weeks ago, I overheard Cora talking on the phone to a friend about an Internet site she often visited to download essays for school papers. "There's no way the teachers can tell it's not your own writing," she'd said.

I am conflicted about what to say and how to vote in the upcoming meeting where new NHS members are determined.

CASE #4

Student: Denise

Brief Biography: Denise is an Anglo, age forty-four, married with two young adult children. She has long volunteered in parish ministry and now would like to be hired by a parish in the diocese, perhaps as a pastoral associate.

Site Description: St. Hedwig's is a midwestern parish originally founded in 1850 by German immigrants. The church holds eight hundred people and, at one point in time, had a school of nine hundred children. Currently, however, there are only two Masses on Sunday, each attended by about 100–150 people. Much of the neighborhood population is African American, but this is not reflected in parish membership. Many of those who attend Mass could be counted among the elderly poor. They are mostly Euro-American.

Many live alone in houses that they have owned for nearly all of their adult lives.

Narrative for Reflection: Each Monday (as part of my learning objective to see up close the administrative work involved in parish leadership), I spend several hours sitting with the parish secretary and bookkeeper. One of the tasks we regularly engage in is receiving and recording Mass stipends. Right at 9 a.m., every Monday, we are visited by Marie, an elderly white woman who lives near the church in a small shotgun house on which the paint is peeling. She wears a tattered coat and struggles to walk with a cane. But every Monday, rain or shine, she comes in to give $20 for Masses for the poor souls in purgatory.

Last week, she mentioned that she has been unable to pay her heating bills for the last two months, but she wants to still give this $20 every week because she knows that the poor souls need help and because she made a vow many years ago to give this money. If she breaks her vow, she believes God will send her to hell when she dies. The parish secretary, an older German woman herself, nodded sympathetically and lamented that so few people remember the poor souls any more. The bookkeeper, who was facing the other direction, rolled her eyes and murmured quietly to me: "Nonsense, but it is the only thing that keeps this parish afloat." I felt very uncomfortable. I was angry with both the secretary and the bookkeeper. I felt very bad for Marie. I felt sorry that her beliefs weighed on her so heavily, but I also sensed that they might be all that were keeping her alive. I also felt awkward because I didn't want to embarrass or contradict the secretary. So I kept quiet, and Marie left.

CASE #5

Student: Fr. Raul

Brief Biography: Raul, age thirty-six, is a religious priest who has been sent by his religious congregation in Belize to pursue a master's degree in liturgy in the United States so that he can teach in the congregation's seminary. While studying, he is living and ministering at Holy Child Parish. He has chosen an off-site supervisor who is a liturgist in a nearby parish to work with him since the pastor is a close friend in the congregation.

Site Description: Holy Child is a large church built to hold nine hundred people, but the best-attended Sunday Mass only draws about three hundred on average, with many people sitting in the back creating a great distance between the presider and the congregation. Holy Child was originally a white, mostly Irish, working-class parish, but over the past fifty years, the number of registered parishioners has dropped significantly and diversified as the neighborhood has changed. Now the parish is about half white and half Vietnamese, Mexican, and Ethiopian.

Narrative for Reflection: I have been asked by the pastor to oversee the coordination of the liturgical life of the parish. This includes working with the liturgy and environment committee—a branch of the parish council. Just before I came, the committee had decided to rope off the back ten pews of the parish church to encourage people to move forward, closer to the front. Many times, it is white parishioners who are sitting in the front and Vietnamese, Mexican, and Ethiopian parishioners who are sitting in the back, though there are also many white parishioners in the back pews. The liturgy committee wanted to help create a more united church by having the people intermingle more and sit closer together. But roping off the back pews has caused an uproar in the parish. The pastor has received numerous complaints, including written ones. One person wrote that he had been a parishioner for fifty years and had put up with all the changes of Vatican II, but that the roping off of his seat had been the last straw, and he was leaving the Church. It seems like right now it is the only thing that people talk about in the parish.

CASE #6

Student: Juana

Brief Biography: Juana is a sixty-year-old woman who was born in Cuba but has lived in the United States since she was seven. She is recently widowed, with three grown children. A lifelong Catholic, she has become more involved in social justice ministry since retiring from her work as a librarian at the city library. She became director of Hosanna House a few months ago, after the sister who started the project retired.

Site Description: Hosanna House is a small social ministry outreach sponsored by a local congregation of women religious. It provides canned goods and used clothing for those in need, evening tutoring to help adults finish a GED, and a day school that helps immigrants learn English.

Narrative for Reflection: This is my fifth month as director at Hosanna House. Besides myself, there is one part-time employee, Monique. She works with me two days a week. She answers requests for assistance and helps bring canned goods and clothing to those who've called asking for help. Monique has been working here for five years. She was originally one of the first clients of this social ministry program but with a lot of help from the sisters was able to pull herself out of poverty and get off welfare. She's been able to buy a car and a small house in the neighborhood for herself and her two sons. She works the other days of the week as the receptionist in a dental office.

A couple times now, I've been with Monique when she has popped open one of the donated canned goods for lunch. And a few times I've seen her rifle through the donated clothing, picking out a few of the nicer items for her son's child to wear. Last week, I found Monique filling a box with a couple bags of chips, saying that she was having a small party that evening and wouldn't have time to make it to the grocery store after work.

I feel so conflicted about the situation, unsure whether to say something to Monique at all, and if so, what.

CASE #7

Student: Marguerite

Brief Biography: Marguerite, age thirty-three and Anglo, is a single lay woman pursuing a master of divinity degree after several years of teaching experience in the Peace Corps in Micronesia. Now in the last year of her studies, she is completing an internship at St. Ferdinand's Parish, a semester-long commitment of fifteen to twenty hours per week.

Site Description: St. Ferdinand's is a small, vibrant city parish in the northern region of the country. It has very active and committed parishioners who take their service to the Church seriously. She is the first intern the pastor has ever supervised. Besides the parish secretary, the maintenance worker, and the parish cook, she is the first lay person on staff.

Narrative for Reflection: I am now in the eighth week of my internship. In my learning contract, I've said that I want to learn in general how a parish runs, observing the variety of different ministries that go on here and getting involved in them as much as possible. I've offered to help with RCIA, but there is only one person in the program, and it seems like overkill to have a group of four well-trained RCIA leaders for one person. The parish's social ministry is well run by volunteers three mornings a week. They don't want to have me open it any more days because what will happen when I leave at the end of the semester? I have gone on a few sick calls with you (the pastor), but most of those people have gotten better. I have a small office on the second floor and even a telephone line, but no one ever calls. I feel increasingly marginalized—entirely peripheral to the life of the parish.

CASE #8

Student: Todd

Brief Biography: Todd is a twenty-nine-year-old, single lay man of second-generation Asian American descent. Following graduation from college, he began working for the university's campus ministry department while working part-time on his master's in pastoral ministry. For several years now, he has facilitated Bible studies, organized service trips to Appalachia, served on retreat teams, etc., with great success. He is using his work at the college as his field placement.

Site Description: Harborough College is a small liberal arts university sponsored by a women's religious congregation in the southeastern United States. With a one-to-twelve faculty-to-student ratio, the school prides itself on its "family feel" and close-knit community. Faculty and students are often on a first-name basis. The campus ministry is the heart of the school. Undergraduate students, graduate students, faculty members, and their families all commonly worship there.

Narrative for Reflection: I love my job, but sometimes it is a little awkward. You see, the students whom I am working with are mostly just a little bit younger than I am, and some are the same age as I am or even older. Over the years, I've grown very close to some of them.

One of the longtime young adult group members, Peter, age twenty-five, just finished law school and passed the state bar. To top it off, he's gotten a job offer from a great law firm in town. To celebrate, he's inviting a couple of guys—mostly other members of the young adult group—to go with him and spend a week at his parent's winter house along the Florida coast. He's invited me to go along. And he's said that if I can't afford the plane fare right now, he'd pay it as a thank-you for "all the times I've been there for him over the years." I would really like to go, but I am not sure whether it is appropriate.

CASE #9

Student: Akinshiju

Brief Biography: "Aki" is a first-year seminarian from Nigeria who has lived in the United States for only a short period of time. He is preparing to serve in a rural U.S. diocese. He is thirty-four years old, of Yoruba ethnicity. He speaks English very well but is challenged by cultural cues. He is in his first field education placement—a nursing home—where he is to visit Catholic residents and bring them communion. He is present in the home about two hours a week.

Site Description: The Serenity Home is a 150-bed nursing home with no religious affiliation, but volunteer chaplains from several denominations make regular visits and are on call should someone request a visit. Once a month, a priest from the local Catholic parish comes to celebrate Eucharist on-site.

Narrative for Reflection: The nursing home makes me very sad every time I visit. It is a very pretty building with many lovely pictures and flowers. But everyone there is so alone. Most people sit alone in their rooms all day without visitors. The nurses and staff members are always very busy, and they never stop to talk with the older people. They just give them their medicine and then go to the next room. Sometimes people wait a long time when they need help.

    Yesterday, I visited Mr. B. He had been sitting in his wheelchair for a long time and wanted to go to bed. He said he had been waiting for almost an hour already when I arrived. You could see he was so tired. I said to him, "I will help you." I helped him to stand up and take just the few steps needed to get into the bed. I took off his shoes and helped him lie down. I took the blanket from the back of the chair and laid it over him. He said, "Thank you so much." I felt so good to be able to help him in this way. I felt like Simon of Cyrene.

CASE #10

Student: Don

Brief Biography: Don is a forty-year-old Anglo who came to the seminary after a successful career in computer programming. He has recently been ordained a transitional deacon and anticipates ordination to the priesthood in a couple of months. He spends three days a week at the parish.

Site Description: Blessed Sacrament is a Catholic parish of five hundred families located in a big college town. The town's life revolves around the college's football team.

Narrative for Reflection: Last Saturday morning, I was alone at the parish center with the exception of Liz, the teenager who answers the phones on weekends. A woman, whom I will call "Mrs. P," came to the door and asked if she could talk to a priest. Liz told her that there were no priests available, but the woman asked if there was *anyone* she could please talk to. Liz called me down. I introduced myself as Deacon Don and agreed to speak with Mrs. P in the spiritual direction room.

As soon as we sat down, Mrs. P began crying and saying that something awful had happened—her nineteen-year-old daughter, "K", had been raped. I asked her to tell me more about what had happened. She said that K had been raped three weeks ago, but that she had only just found out about it. K had been at a bar that some of the college football players frequented. She'd had a crush on one of the football players all season and was flirting with him in the bar. The athlete said that the bar was too smoky and loud to talk much and invited K outside to the back parking lot. Once in the parking lot, they began kissing, and then he started fondling K and pressing himself on her. K tried to resist, but he wouldn't stop, and he raped her. I asked Mrs. P, "Are you sure there was penetration?" and she said, "Yes."

I asked her if K was okay now. She said, "I guess so. I made her take a pregnancy test, and she is not pregnant." But she said that K was still withdrawn and crying a lot.

Then I asked Mrs. P if she was married. She said that she was, but that there was no way she could tell her husband about this because if she did, he would be very angry with K and would try to kill the football player. I asked if anyone else knew, and she said that her friend Mrs. W knew and had told her to come and talk to the priest.

I let her know again that I wasn't a priest yet and that I couldn't hear confession or absolve her. She told me that she didn't want confession; she wanted me to do something about the situation. She told me that she had the number of the football player. I asked her what she wanted me to do. She said she wanted me to go to the coach of the football team and tell him what the football player had done and stop him from doing it again.

I told her that I couldn't do that. "Why?" she asked. I told her that I had heard only her side of the story and not K's. I said that I'd need to hear the facts from K before I could do anything else.

Mrs. P, who had stopped crying, started crying again and became angry. "Are you saying that you are not going to help us?" she shouted. I said that I couldn't do anything more without K's permission and that I'd need to talk to K directly. I gave Mrs. P the parish card and wrote my name on it and told her to have K call and ask for me. Mrs. P took the card and put it into her pocket. She pursed her lips and said, "Thank you, Deacon." She walked out of the room and slammed the door. I haven't heard from Mrs. P or K since.

Sample Supervisor Case Studies

In field education, it is not only students who find themselves in the midst of situations meriting theological reflection. Supervisors, too, may have cases of their own worthy of reflection, either personally or with a peer group of supervisors. Consider each of the following situations from the perspective of the supervisor. How would you address the matter presented? What sorts of questions would you ask yourself to come to a decision? What resources (persons, texts, etc.) would you want to access to help work through the situation?

CASE #1

Your supervisee, Angie (age twenty-six), is a novice with a local congregation of women religious. Her novice directors note that she is very shy and has "lived a sheltered life" in a rural community. They would like her to get more experience working with people in poverty and so have suggested that she serve in the food pantry that you oversee. Angie is very faithful to showing up on time weekly, but she spends most of her time rearranging cans in the back room and seems hesitant to engage the clients of the pantry. When you ask her to see a client, she becomes very nervous and speaks in such a quiet voice that the clients often do not understand what she is saying. She often casts her eyes down, rather than looking clients in the face. Her organizational skills are excellent, but she doesn't seem to like being with people.

CASE #2

Joy (age twenty-nine) is a fireball of energy and charisma. Everything that she does at the parish is exceedingly well received by the parishioners. She has numerous ideas for how things could be improved or run more smoothly, and she has the ability to carry them out almost effortlessly. She works hard. She is very responsible. She is generous with her time, but also seems to have good boundaries. In fact, she is so successful at what she does that sometimes you wonder whether you have anything to offer her.

CASE #3

Bernardo (age thirty-four) is an intelligent seminarian from the Philippines who arrived in the United States three years ago. When he is scheduled to preach in your parish community, he takes a great deal of time to get ready. He exegetes fastidiously, always has something worthwhile to say, and practices in front of the mirror. Unfortunately, the people in the parish can't understand him because his mastery of spoken English is poor. He also reads the full text of the preaching directly from a paper and avoids looking up at the congregation. Several parishioners have complained to you. Some people arrange to go to other liturgies when they find out he is preaching.

CASE #4

Maeve (age twenty-four) is interested in being a chaplain and has shown great potential thus far during her field placement in your hospital's pediatric cancer ward. A survivor of childhood leukemia herself, she relates well with the young patients, and the staff finds her to be friendly and responsible. You are a little embarrassed, however, by the way that she comes dressed to the site. She often wears jeans and a T-shirt when there is an unspoken expectation for more professional dress. You never introduced a dress code at the beginning of the placement and thought that after a couple of weeks, she would pick up on how everyone else was dressed. You sometimes wonder whether she even has any professional clothing and whether, as a full-time student, she could afford to buy any. You aren't quite sure whether to bring up the topic of dress code at all or just let it slide.

CASE #5

You were thrilled when Bill (age fifty-five) offered to take over the youth group in the parish. It took a great weight off your shoulders, and he seemed to bring many new ideas. Over the past several months, however, participation in the group has steadily declined. Whereas once there were twenty to twenty-five teens showing up at youth group events, now there are only six to eight. When you've casually chatted with some of the teens, they tell you that they find Bill patronizing and boring. They say that he likes to lecture about church teachings rather than discussing them and that he doesn't really understand their lives and problems. He tries to cram too many educational activities into their sessions, they report, and doesn't let them just talk and have fun with one another. When Bill reports to theological reflection, though, he always comes with glowing reports about how well the group is going and how much he enjoys the teens.

CASE #6

Terry (age fifty-two) is a candidate for the permanent diaconate. His field work at the maximum security prison this year has been exceptional. He comes every Tuesday morning for several hours, and then after lunch the two of you meet for theological reflection. The men enjoy his visits and look forward to his coming. One of them chose Terry to accompany him during his last months on death row. Sometimes when you meet with Terry for theological reflection, however, you think you smell alcohol on his breath. At other times, you've thought that the power of his cologne might overwhelm you. Once he seemed to have a case of the "shakes," and he was having a hard time holding his pen steady as he took notes. You wonder whether and how to test your intuition that Terry is an active alcoholic and, since he is doing a good job at his ministry, whether it is even any of your business.

CASE #7

Paula (age forty-eight) has chosen to complete her field placement in the hospice program that you serve. Paula was her mother's primary caretaker during a four-year bout with lung cancer that ended last year. During this time, she was deeply affected by the hospice chaplain who worked with her and her mother and decided that she, too, wanted to be a hospice chaplain. During theological reflection sessions with Paula, you notice how much Paula talks about her mom and her own grieving process. You are concerned that she may be doing the same with the patients. Yesterday, when you passed by a room in which Paula was visiting a patient, your fears were confirmed when you heard her tearfully relating the loss of her mother and saw the patient patting Paula on the hand.

CASE #8

Gregory (age twenty-eight) is a transitional deacon. He has been placed with your parish for the final months before his ordination to the priesthood. He has been an energetic, fresh presence in the parish, launching new efforts to reach out to young adults. He has also been a hit with some of the elderly members of the parish who enjoy his more traditional, clerical approach and willingness to rejuvenate some older devotions that have fallen by the wayside. However, he has not cultivated a good working relationship with the other parish staff members, whom he sometimes treats like subordinates. In particular, he has been dismissive of Pam (age sixty), who has been the parish liturgist for many years.

Pam has no formal theological education but possesses a deep love of liturgy and a natural sense of how to help people worship. Gregory finds Pam consistently inattentive to some of the finer details of the *General Instruction on the Roman Missal*. On occasion, he has corrected her publicly, and she has expressed how embarrassed she was. Pam tells you that if Gregory continues to treat her like a child, she will resign from the staff. Gregory tells you that if the parish's liturgy is not brought into full conformity with the *GIRM*, he thinks that in good conscience he must inform the bishop.

CASE #9

Hector (age twenty-nine) is a religious brother in temporary profession, trying to discern whether to remain a brother or seek ordination. He has made outstanding contributions to the Hispanic Ministry Office, which you oversee, while modeling true servant leadership. Having come to this country as a young child, he has great empathy for immigrants and is deeply committed to meeting their needs. You really believe he has a call to this ministry and wish you could clone him.

You live about a half hour from the office in a trendy part of town where there are many bars and restaurants and dance clubs frequented by young adults. A few times now, when walking down the street, you have passed by a bar well known in the neighborhood to be a gay bar and seen Hector inside having a drink with friends. Last week, when the weather turned warmer, he was sitting on the outdoor patio of the bar, smoking a cigarette and drinking a martini with one other male. When you walked by, your eyes met and you decided to stop and greet him. Hector politely greeted you, but blushed a bit and hesitated to introduce his tablemate. You are not sure how, or even whether, to follow up on the incident.

CASE #10

Bobbie (age fifty-three) has been a great assistance in visiting and bringing communion to parishioners who are homebound and in local nursing homes. The elderly parishioners love being visited and enjoy the home-baked cookies that she often brings. Unfortunately, she drives you batty. You find her loud and overbearing. Her high-pitched laugh shreds your nerves. She frequently calls you "a dear thing" and "honey." Every time she comes for supervision, she brings you a little gift from her kitchen, even though you have said several times that she really shouldn't. You feel mothered by her in a way that makes you feel like you are back at home rather than in a professional relationship. There really is nothing wrong with her ministry, but the supervisory relationship itself feels awkward and grating.

CASE #11

Dave (age thirty-four) is in his last semester of studies, and graduation is so close that he can taste it. Dave has a three-year-old and just found out that his wife is pregnant again with twins. She's held down a part-time job these past three years so that Dave could get his master of divinity, something he's dreamed of doing since he left the seminary. But now with severe morning sickness, she hasn't been able to work, and Dave has had to keep up with a full-time load of courses while helping out more at home and taking up some odd jobs on the side. Dave is supposed to be completing a final internship this semester at your site, but he hasn't been very faithful to showing up for all of his hours. He frequently comes unprepared to theological reflection. He didn't show up at all the week of midterms because he had some kind of major senior synthesis project to finish for a class. His hair is starting to visibly gray at the edges, and he just keeps saying, "Only eight more weeks and this craziness will all be over."

A Self-Assessment for Supervisors

In field education, students are often asked to assess themselves as ministers, identifying their strengths and areas for growth. Supervisors are not often asked to engage in the same sort of self-assessment of their supervisory ministry but can derive great benefit from doing so. The following is one possible tool to be used in supervisory self-assessment. Using a scale of 1 to 5, with 1 indicating a serious weakness and 5 indicating a great strength, respond to each of the following statements. Identify a few areas that you would like to be especially attentive to in developing yourself as a supervisor. What strategies might help you to do so? If possible, discuss with other supervisors who may be able to offer ideas.

Professional Competency

_____ I possess the theological knowledge and understanding needed to help students converse meaningfully about their ministerial experiences from a faith perspective.

_____ I possess a basic understanding of human and spiritual development and how these impact a person's capacities for ministry.

_____ I possess sufficient competency in my own area of ministry to be initiating another into the ministry.

_____ I understand the learning methodology of field education and feel comfortable shepherding a student through field education processes (e.g., learning contracts, evaluations, lay committees, etc.).

_____ I am aware of the ministry program's goals for its field education component and am able to commit myself to help reaching those goals.

_____ I am aware of indications of unsuitability for ministry and know what to do when I see such indications.

_____ I know how to refer a student to resources for counseling or spiritual direction as needed.

_____ I am familiar with the ethical issues that can surface in a supervisory relationship and, in particular, any code of ethics that the ministry program might establish for its supervisors and students.

_____ I have healthy boundaries and know when and how to say "no."

_____ While maintaining boundaries, I am still accessible and approachable; I also know how to say "yes."

_____ I am able to observe confidentiality; I know what to keep confidential and what needs to be reported to a field education or program director.

_____ I know what my own personal issues and agendas are, and I avoid projecting them onto the students.

_____ I am able to commit to the time required to supervise a ministry student.

_____ I am able to regularly meet the deadlines and expectations of the field education program.

_____ I am faithful to commitments that I've made; I follow through on things I've said I'd do.

_____ I have a good sense about when it would be appropriate to wait and observe and when it would be appropriate to be proactive and speak to a student.

_____ In my regular ministry, I model the kind of ministry that I would want my student to be able to imitate, especially in respect to

    _____ how I treat those to whom I minister

    _____ how I treat fellow staff members

    _____ how I treat those to whom I am accountable

    _____ how I talk about the larger Church

    _____ how I manage and balance my time and personal needs

    _____ how I steward my resources

    _____ how I handle conflicts

    _____ the importance of a prayer life

Ministerial Identity and Authority

_____ I believe I have wrestled with questions of ministerial identity myself and know something about how to help students work through these questions.

_____ I have a strong sense of being called to the ministry of supervision.

_____ I feel comfortable with students regarding me as a supervisor.

_____ I possess a strong pastoral presence in supervisory ministry that is marked by
    _____ excellent listening skills
    _____ comfort with silence
    _____ ability to display empathy and compassion
    _____ ability to be present to a student who is grieving or angry.
    _____ ability to serve with a certain objectivity students who hold different theological or political perspectives than I do
    _____ ability to serve students of another gender, ethnicity, or sexual orientation

_____ I possess a strong prophetic presence in supervisory ministry that is marked by
    _____ ability to confront injustice, irresponsibility, error, or ignorance
    _____ ability to offer constructive criticism
    _____ ability to successfully negotiate conflict
    _____ acceptance of the challenges of the ministry
    _____ endurance and faithfulness

_____ I am capable of making decisions, even under stress, even when they do not make all people happy.

_____ I have a good understanding of what healthy authority looks like.

_____ I am unafraid to possess authority and speak with authority.

_____ I have a healthy relationship with those in authority within civil society and within the Church.

_____ I am capable of sharing authority and empowering others for leadership.

_____ I am a "transparent" person; my public persona is not disconnected from my private persona.

_____ I exercise appropriate self-disclosure; I know what to share of myself and (where applicable) my family or community life, as well as what not to share.

_____ I am a person of prayer and am comfortable leading others in public prayer.

_____ My choices consider the communal impact that a decision will make, not only the personal impact.

Habit of Theological Reflection

_____ I see how the theology I have studied connects to everyday life and how everyday life can raise theological questions.

_____ I find myself spontaneously making theological connections in ministry.

_____ Theological reflection is a personal habit that I am committed to in my own life.

_____ I feel comfortable facilitating others in theological reflection.

_____ I possess a basic understanding of cultural and social analysis that enriches theological reflection.

_____ I understand the ways in which the following affect the ministry I do
_____ my family history
_____ my personality
_____ my gender and sexual orientation
_____ my ethnicity
_____ my personal life experience

_____ I feel competent helping others see the way in which these same factors in their lives affect the way they do ministry.

_____ I am able to think symbolically—to bring a broad range of images from life, scripture, and history to theological reflection.

_____ I do ongoing reading and study in the areas of theology, scripture, social sciences, etc., to continue enriching my theological reflection and the theological reflection that I do with others.

Praying With Images of Supervision

One of the best ways to honor the spiritually transformative potential of supervision is to pray with various images from scripture that capture an aspect of the supervisor's vocation. The following scripture passages do not model a professional supervisory relationship, but each of them has been helpful to other supervisors in illuminating or mirroring a facet of the supervisory relationship as they have experienced it.

As you are supervising, perhaps you will want to choose one of the following passages—or another of your own choosing—at the beginning of each month to reflect upon further. Some of the passages are quite long and may need to be spread out over the course of the month. Others are shorter and could be read several times periodically throughout the month. At the end of the month, spend time journaling about connections that you have discovered. Or gather with other supervisors to talk about insights you have gleaned.

Suggested Scripture Passages

1 Samuel 3:1–18 *Eli helps Samuel discern God's call. Samuel hears a message he would rather not share with Eli.*

2 Samuel 12:1–13 *The prophet Nathan puts a mirror before David in the form of a story.*

1 Kings 19:19–21; 2 Kings 2:1–14 *Elijah passes on the prophet's mantle to Elisha.*

Tobit 5:4–6:1 *Tobiah meets a disguised angel who will accompany him to Media and introduce many surprises along the way.*

Matthew 15:21–28 or Mark 7:24–30 *Jesus understands his own call and ministry better after being challenged by a Canaanite woman.*

Luke 1:39–56 *Mary and Elizabeth share with each other the amazing things that God is doing in their lives.*

Luke 24:13–27 *Two disciples on the way to Emmaus are pondering the events surrounding Jesus' death when the Risen Christ draws alongside them on the road and helps them look at the story they were telling in a new way.*

John 2:1–11 *Mary pushes Jesus to do something about the wine shortage at a wedding in Cana and encourages others to trust his leadership. In doing so, she opens the door to his public ministry.*

John 4:4–30 *Jesus engages in an eye-opening, truth-filled conversation with a Samaritan woman he meets at the well.*

John 13:1–15 *In the washing of the feet, Jesus sets a model of ministerial behavior for those he has mentored to follow in his footsteps.*

Acts 5:36–37; 9:23–28; 11:19–30; 13:1–15:41 *Barnabas, the "Son of Encouragement," takes the new convert Paul and shepherds him into the Christian community and into ministry. Eventually Paul takes on more of a leadership role and Barnabas less so, until the two finally go separate ways.*

Acts 18:1–4, 18–27 *Aquila and Priscilla provide hospitality in their home to Paul and later to Apollos, providing each with the nurturing needed for the next part of his ministry.*

Questions for Reflection and Discussion or Journaling

1. What aspect of the relationship present in this passage reminds you of supervision or challenges you as a supervisor?
2. What in the passage is unlike or different from your experience of the ministry of supervision?
3. Is there a phrase or an idea from the passage that leaps out to you and that you want to ruminate upon for a while longer?
4. If you were to ask the person playing the role of "supervisor" in this passage for advice, what would the person say to you? If you were to request a gift from this person that would help you to be a better supervisor, for what would you ask?
5. If the "supervisor" in the passage were to offer a prayer to God on your behalf, what would you want him or her to pray?

Relevant Ecclesial Documents Concerning Ministerial Field Education

John Paul II, *I Will Give You Shepherds* **(***Pastores Dabo Vobis***), March 25, 1992.** *Pastores Dabo Vobis* is an apostolic exhortation prepared by John Paul II on the formation of priests for the modern age. It is the document upon which the fifth edition of the *Program of Priestly Formation* is based. The key section regarding field education is found in #58.

> And so pastoral formation certainly cannot be reduced to a mere apprenticeship, aiming to make the candidate familiar with some pastoral techniques. The seminary [that] educates must seek really and truly to initiate the candidate into the sensitivity of being a shepherd, in the conscious and mature assumption of his responsibilities, in the interior habit of evaluating problems and establishing priorities and looking for solutions on the basis of honest motivations of faith and according to the theological demands inherent in pastoral work.

Thanks to an initial and gradual experience of ministry, future priests will be able to be inserted into the living pastoral tradition of their particular church. . . . They will get practice in some initial forms of cooperation with one another and with the priests alongside whom they will be sent to work. These priests have a considerably important role, in union with the seminary program, in showing the candidates how they should go about pastoral work. When it comes to choosing places and services in which candidates can obtain their pastoral experience, the parish should be given particular importance, for it is a living cell of local and specialized pastoral work in which they will find themselves faced with the kind of problems they will meet in their future ministry. The synod fathers have proposed a number of concrete examples such as visits to the sick; caring for immigrants, refugees, and nomads; and various social works, which can be expressions of charitable zeal.

United States Conference of Catholic Bishops, *Program of Priestly Formation*, **fifth edition, November 15, 2005.** The *Program of Priestly Formation* (*PPF*) guides seminaries in designing holistic programs for the formation of Roman Catholic priests. The formation is structured around four pillars: human formation, spiritual formation, intellectual formation, and pastoral formation. The pastoral formation section of the document is quite lengthy, encompassing numbers 236 through 257. Field education is understood to be one of the key methods of pastoral formation. Written largely for a diocesan context, *PPF* notes that much of seminarians' pastoral experience should take place in the context of a parish. It also suggests that seminarians be placed in a variety of different settings during their formation, including settings with great cultural and ethnic diversity, settings that offer opportunities to work with and for the poor, and ecumenical and interreligious settings engaged in social action and outreach. It urges that all seminarians be trained to serve as "shepherds" in the Church—a role that requires formation in all of the following areas:

- effective communication of God's Word
- sacramental celebration
- missionary activity
- care and guidance of a community
- flexibility of spirit
- synthesis of theological knowledge with personal experience
- cultural sensitivity
- ministering in a pluralistic context
- effective and meaningful collaboration with fellow priests, religious, professional lay ministers, parish councils, etc.
- knowledge of the poor and the issues and structures that affect their lives
- leadership development

While field education is not the sole means by which these areas of pastoral formation are addressed, it is implied that many of these areas can be practiced, reflected upon, and evaluated through field placements.

Select paragraphs regarding field education supervision, theological reflection, and evaluation are included here:

#239[7]

An initiation to various practical, pastoral experiences, especially in parishes: It is important not to sacrifice human, spiritual, and intellectual formation for practical experience. Still, it is essential to cultivate pastoral formation and to enhance and integrate the other dimensions of formation so that the seminarian has opportunities to experience pastoral life firsthand. Seminaries have initiated students into pastoral experiences and reflection on them in a variety of ways: concurrent field placements, pastoral quarters or internships, clinical pastoral education, and diaconate internships. Whatever the setting, it is necessary that it facilitate learning. It is also necessary that there be a guide, mentor, or teacher who accompanies the student and helps him to learn from the experience. In addition, there should be a priest supervisor who helps the student enter into the specifically priestly dimension of the ministry. In these experiences, the student first enters the scene as an observer, then raises questions to understand what is happening, and finally relates it to his other formation. He ought then to practice or try to do what the situation requires. After that, he can profit from supervision that helps him to assess what happened and gives him feedback. A process of theological reflection follows that identifies the faith assumptions and convictions underlying both the situation and the ministerial response. Theological reflection thus provides an opportunity for personal synthesis, the clarification of motivations, and the development of directions for life and ministry. And the final step, of course, is in fact to return to the ministry or pastoral situation, but now with more knowledge and ability and a better inner sense of direction because of an enriched spiritual life and a more deeply grounded sense of priestly identity. It is the responsibility of the diocesan bishop, religious ordinary, and the rectors to ensure that the Catholic, sacramental dimension of pastoral care is integral to all such programs in which seminarians participate.

#240

Pastoral formation depends in great measure on the quality of supervision. To serve as a supervisor of seminarians calls for experience, competence, and generosity. Priests and others who serve as supervisors, mentors, and teachers are an extension of the faculty of the seminary. It is important that this identification with priestly formation become part of the mindset of pastoral staffs that serve to initiate seminarians to pastoral life. When onsite pastoral formation is seen as an integral part of priestly formation, then pastoral staffs must accept a special responsibility in the name of the Church for the direction and help they provide to seminarians. These priests and those associated with them must have certain qualities that include loyal commitment to priestly formation, patience, honesty, an almost instinctive way of thinking theologically in pastoral situations, and a habit of prayer that permeates the ministry.

#248

Supervision, theological reflection, and evaluation are necessary components of an effective pastoral program. Although theological reflection can help the development of pastoral skills, its primary purpose is to interpret pastoral experience or activity in light of Scripture, church teaching, personal faith, and pastoral practices. Reflection of this kind should become a lifelong habit in priestly ministry.

#249

Onsite supervisors should be carefully selected with an eye to their dedication to the Church and respect for the priesthood. They should be taught the skills of pastoral supervision and evaluation. In choosing pastoral internships and summer placements and their supervisors, bishops and vocation personnel should consider carefully the particular needs of individual seminarians and the available time and supervisory skills of the supervisors.

#250

In addition to onsite supervisors, others collaborating in the various ministries, as well as those served, should be asked to participate in the evaluation of seminarians in ministry.

United States Council of Catholic Bishops, *National Directory for the Formation, Ministry, and Life of Permanent Deacons in the United States,* **December 26, 2004.** The *National Directory* establishes norms for the formation of Roman Catholic deacons. Like The *Program of Priestly Formation,* it encourages the practice of placing those preparing for ordination to the diaconate in a variety of different settings to gain pastoral experience during their formation, but with a special emphasis on non-parish sites. Pastoral formation for the deacon, it urges, should focus on the diakonia or service of the Word, the liturgy, charity, and justice. Later, the document mentions that in many cases it would be suitable to gain deeper experience in one field of ministry, such as catechetics or pastoral counseling.

Select paragraphs follow:

#126

An integral formation must relate the human, spiritual, and intellectual dimensions to pastoral practice. "The whole formation imparted to [the participants] . . . aims at preparing them to enter into communion with the charity of Christ. . . . Hence their formation in its different aspects must have a fundamentally pastoral character." Within that context, the pastoral dimension in formation is not merely an apprenticeship to familiarize the participant in diaconal formation with some pastoral techniques. Its aim, however, is to initiate the aspirant and candidate into the sensitivity of what it means to be a disciple of Jesus, who came to serve and not be served. Pastoral field education embodies this orientation, promoting learning through active engagement in a pastoral situation. Pastoral field education fosters a general integration in the formational process, forging a close link between the human, spiritual, and intellectual dimensions in formation. Evangelization; Catholic schools; catechetics; religious education; youth ministry, social justice outreach opportunities; rural ministry; ecumenism; the care of the sick, elderly, and dying; as well as service opportunities in varied cultural settings indicate the breadth of experiences to which an aspirant and candidates may be exposed in the course of his pastoral field education program.

#127

The pastoral dimension in diaconal formation should strengthen and enhance the exercise of the prophetic, priestly, and servant-leadership functions—deriving from his baptismal consecration—already lived and exercised by the participant in diaconal formation. In each path in formation, they must be taught how to proclaim the Christian message and teach it, how to lead others in communal celebrations of liturgical prayer, and how to witness to the Church in a Christian service marked by charity and justice. The demonstration of pastoral skills is a crucial element in the assessment of fitness for ordination. Therefore, the qualities to be developed for these tasks are as follows: a spirit of pastoral responsibility and servant-leadership; generosity and perseverance; creativity; respect for ecclesial communion; and filial obedience to the bishop. Through his participation in pastoral field education, the participant should have a genuine confidence in his abilities and a realistic sense of his limitations.

#128

Pastoral formation should take into account that those preparing for the diaconate have already been involved in the mission of the Church. The pastoral field education program should be designed, therefore, to build upon previous experiences and talents already displayed. In addition to identifying and developing the gifts already at work, the pastoral dimension of formation should aim at helping the participant to discover talents, perhaps unrecognized, and to develop the skills necessary for exercising the threefold diaconal ministry. A participant needs to demonstrate a genuine confidence in his own ability—a realistic sense of achieving the knowledge and skills required for an effective diaconal ministry—and a strong desire to serve in a broad range of ministerial circumstances.

#131

As part of his pastoral field education formation, the candidate should acquire an appropriate multicultural awareness, exposure, and sensitivity, suitable to the needs of the diocese, including the possibility of learning a second language and studying its cultural context.

#133

Pastoral formation must include theological reflection so the participant may integrate his ministerial activity with the broad scope of diaconal studies. This process should lead him to a lifelong effort in reflecting on his ministry in the light of faith.

#219

During formation, engagement in a wide diversity of pastoral field education placements, at least on a limited basis, will not only give the candidate a greater awareness of the needs and mission of the [diocesan] Church, but will assist in the discernment and development of his own . . . talents and gifts. These pastoral field education experiences should provide an opportunity for theological reflection, as well as occasions to translate intellectual knowledge into pastoral service. . . . Competent, objective, and supportive supervisors will be required in order to achieve these goals. The diocesan Church must be committed to the [selection and] preparation of skillful . . . supervisors who possess pastoral experience, [training] . . . in the art of supervision, and . . . [the ability to assist] mature men with [diverse] life experiences. . . . During candidacy, emphasis also should be given to the study of the role of culture in human, spiritual, and pastoral formation. Further, the pastoral dimension should provide a significant grounding in the social justice teaching of the Church.

#220

A primary opportunity for assessment of the candidate would be within an actual pastoral setting. Can the candidate do that which his training is preparing him to do? Does the way in which he presents himself in pastoral ministry show, for example, an integrated and balanced sense of the ecclesiology of the Second Vatican Council and an understanding of his role within the Church and in its mission of service? Does the way he participates in and leads prayerful gatherings of his community give evidence of liturgical knowledge and cultural sensitivity? Can he demonstrate a properly formed conscience and moral sensitivity? Can he form others in a convincing, sound manner?

#221

Another assessment option is theological reflection on his pastoral practice. Here the role of the peer community is of utmost importance.

The candidate reports on his field education experience, and the community enables him to reflect upon the human, spiritual, intellectual, and pastoral dimensions of his actions. This format greatly fosters the sense of partnership in assessment.

United States Conference of Catholic Bishops, *Co-Workers in the Vineyard of the Lord: A Resource for Guiding the Development of Lay Ecclesial Ministry,* **November 2005.** *Co-Workers in the Vineyard,* unlike The *Program of Priestly Formation* or *National Directory for the Formation, Ministry, and Life of Permanent Deacons,* does not establish norms or particular law. However, it does offer reflection on what has been learned about the best practices for forming lay ecclesial ministers in the United States since the Second Vatican Council. Based on a four-pillar structure similar to the documents on the formation of priests and deacons, it locates field education under pastoral formation. While it doesn't speak about where field placements should take place or who should supervise lay ministry students, it does advocate for field education and lists a lengthy number of areas in which lay ecclesial ministers should become competent, including (among others) methods of forming others, leading community prayer and preaching, pastoral ministry skills, effective relationship and communication skills, collaboration, volunteer management, change and conflict management, basic counseling, appropriate cultural and language skills, leadership and organizational development, and administration. Relevant paragraphs from the document follow:

> *Faith sharing and theological reflection.* Sharing faith among program participants provides mutual support and encouragement and builds bonds

of community. Theological reflection, which is more systematic and comprehensive, attends to experience in the light of faith, culture, and the teaching of the Church and helps participants to recognize the movement of God in their lives and ministry (p. 42).

Methods of Pastoral Formation. The knowledge, skills, and attitudes necessary for pastoral ministry may be taught in traditional classroom or seminar formats, but that is not enough. The teaching must be supplemented by practical experience in real situations and by mentored reflection on those experiences. These experiences include opportunities to practice skills with feedback, as well as demonstrations, projects and practica, and role playing (p. 49).

Although the four elements of formation (human, spiritual, intellectual, and pastoral) have been addressed separately, they must be integrated as a unified whole in the person of the well-formed lay ecclesial minister, which happens best if these elements are integrated in the formation program itself.

Such integration can be fostered through *guided pastoral practice*—field experience or a practicum requiring the learner to put into practice what has been learned, drawing consciously on all four dimensions of formation in planning, implementing, and evaluating a project of ministerial service. The role of the mentor or supervisor is essential here, guiding the learner to reflect upon, understand, and grow from the lived experience of ministry (p. 50).

United States Conference of Catholic Bishops Commission on Certification and Accreditation, *Accreditation Handbook for Ministry Formation Programs,* **March 2003.** The USCCB Commission on Certification and Accreditation establishes accreditation standards, policies, and procedures and accredits quality ministry formation programs sponsored by institutions listed in *The Official Catholic Directory.* Relevant paragraphs follow:

3.4 The curriculum shall provide regular opportunities for participants to learn and to practice the art of theological reflection.

3.6 The curriculum shall provide opportunities for participants to learn about and to practice the skills or activities needed for competency in ministry, including:

3.6.1 Understanding the principles of ongoing faith development and spiritual growth;

3.6.2 Understanding and using the principles of designing and leading public prayer;

3.6.3 Practicing the skills for communicating one-on-one, the skills of public speaking, and the intercultural communication skills based on an awareness of personal cultural identity;

3.6.4 Knowing and using the skills for planning and organizing projects and events;

3.6.5 Knowing and using the skills for facilitating meetings;

3.6.6 Knowing the skills for motivating involvement based on the call of baptism and the ecclesial elements of ministry;

3.6.7 Knowing and using the skills for inviting, training, supervising, evaluating, and offering support to those who contribute their service;

3.6.8 Knowing and practicing conflict management skills;

3.6.9 Knowing and practicing skills of self-reflection and being able to articulate ministerial strengths and limitations, feelings, attitudes, values, and assumptions that affect ministry;

3.6.10 Knowing the behaviors that evidence psychological and ministerial maturity; and

3.6.11 Understanding the role of the public, commissioned, or certified ecclesial minister.

3.7 The curriculum shall provide participants with an experience of a supervised ministry practicum that includes the following elements:

3.7.1 The necessary information and skills for participants to minister effectively in their chosen practicum;

3.7.2 An opportunity to formulate personal goals and objectives in a signed learning agreement;

3.7.3 Opportunities to meet regularly and receive ongoing supervision during the practicum;

3.7.4 Opportunities to meet with peers for support during the practicum; and

3.7.5 Opportunities to be evaluated during and after the practicum by supervisors, mentors, parish staff, parochial vicars, pastors, or chief administrators of the ministry site.

Ann M. Garrido teaches at Aquinas Institute of Theology in St. Louis, directing the doctoral program in preaching and the masters program in the Catechesis of the Good Shepherd. Prior to that, she served for seven years as the Director of Field Education and Assistant Professor of Pastoral Theology there. An active member of the Catholic Association for Theological Field Education, she served as the steering committee chair of the organization from 2004–2006. Ann is the co-editor of *The Theology of Priesthood* and author of *Mustard Seed Preaching*. She has spoken widely on the topics of ministry formation and theological reflection in diocesan, academic, and health care settings.

THE CONCISE GUIDE SERIES

The books of *The Concise Guide Series*, edited by Kevin McKenna, tackle questions of central importance for contemporary Catholicism. The series offers excellent reference as each book carefully outlines the issues, references the necessary documents, and sketches answers to pressing pastoral questions in highly accessible language and easily understood formats. Glossaries, diagrams, and up-to-date bibliographies are all regular features of these pastorally sensitive and doctrinally sound resources.

 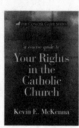  

A Concise Guide to Pastoral Planning
Dr. William Pickett
ISBN: 9781594711350 / 256 pages / $16.95

A Concise Guide to Your Rights in the Catholic Church
Kevin E. McKenna
ISBN: 9781594710798 / 128 pages / $12.95

A Concise Guide to Catholic Social Teaching
Kevin E. McKenna
ISBN: 9780877939795 / 160 pages / $13.95

A Concise Guide to Canon Law
A Practical Handbook for Pastoral Ministers
Kevin E. McKenna
ISBN: 9780877939344 / 128 pages / $12.95

TOGETHER in MINISTRY

ave maria press
Notre Dame, IN 46556
www.avemariapress.com • Ph: 800-282-1865
A Ministry of the Indiana Province of Holy Cross
Available from your local bookstore or from ave maria press

Keycode: FD9Ø6Ø8ØØØØ